What people are say

"There are travel blogs and there are daily devotionals, but what a rare delight to imaginatively walk with Kim through the streets of Paris while reflecting upon the presence and goodness of God in our lives, no matter where our feet may take us. Her well-crafted descriptions and historical narrative enrich the backdrop of her days spent in Paris as her subtle humour engages the reader easily with the experiences she shares. Those stories are enriched as she draws fresh insight and needed reminders from the Scriptures into the overriding journey of what it means to be a disciple of Christ."

Faye Reynolds
Director of Women and Intergenerational Ministries
Canadian Baptists of Western Canada

"It was refreshing to read Kim's writing. Her everyday language, powerful metaphors mixed with descriptive images caused me to often feel like I was there. My senses could almost smell the blossoms or hear the street noise, though I've never been to Paris. Kim has found ways to say complex things, to explore intricate truths with simple and inviting language. She wonders, questions, ponders and finds herself arriving at some understanding without being prescriptive. Like I said, refreshing."

Joline Olson
Teacher
Calgary Christian School

The French *Collection*

Moments with God in Paris

Laurie
Hope you enjoy
these stories!
God bless.
Kim Louise Clarke

Kim Louise Clarke

THE FRENCH COLLECTION
Copyright © 2016 by Kim Louise Clarke

Photos by Kim Louise Clarke

Printed in Canada

ISBN: 978-1-4866-1128-7

Word Alive Press
131 Cordite Road, Winnipeg, MB R3W 1S1
www.wordalivepress.ca

MIX
Paper from
responsible sources
FSC® C016245

WORD ALIVE
—P R E S S—

Cataloguing in Publication may be obtained through Library and Archives Canada

In memory of my mom,
Charlotte Brann,
who loved me and who stepped out in faith

Contents

Acknowledgements

God has surrounded me with remarkable people. I am so thankful for the endless encouragement and constant love from my husband Ian, my daughter Hannah, and my son Philip. They, and my three step-sons, Jeremy, Jamie and Leigh, all demonstrate every day to me that a path taken requires steadfastness. It is one step at a time. I am thankful for my sister Marquita and her bright and encouraging words. I am grateful for the support shown me by my wonderful church family, Crescent Heights Baptist Church and its "1212" Ministries. I treasure my connections with InScribe Christian Writers' Fellowship. Thank you also to Word Alive Press for all their help, advice and encouragement with this publication.

Paris from Notre-Dame Cathedral

Getting There

"He who is outside his door
already has the hardest part of
his journey behind him."
Dutch Proverb

"The World is a book,
and those who do not travel
read only a page."
Saint Augustine

"If at some point you don't ask yourself,
'What have I gotten myself into?',
then you're not doing it right."
Roland Gau

*M*y mom used to say that a vacation that started off badly would be a great trip. I never took this seriously, and certainly never purposefully attempted to do something foolish before a trip if nothing bad had yet happened. I also do not remember her saying this after she became a Christian, and not surprisingly, I can't find any Scripture to substantiate this idea.

It was a few days before I flew to Paris, and my feet were resting comfortably in bubbling, silky warm waters: I had finally used my gift certificate for a pedicure. From the wide selection of colours, I chose a deep pink called 'Bijou', which is French for 'jewel'. My silky smooth feet would soon be strolling around the exotic streets of Paris.

With a sense of enchantment, I stepped back out into the shopping mall but the feeling of specialness quickly began to fade as the tinges of a migraine that had been lurking around the back of my head grew painfully obvious.

I took meds but they proved ineffective and, as I passed a few stores, every movement emphasized the headache's onset. I began to feel extremely ill. While I made my way over to one of the comfortable chairs clustered throughout the mall, I dug out my cell phone to tell my husband that I didn't think I could drive home. A prisoner now in my favourite mall, I sank low in the huge chair, convinced I'd either pass out or vomit if I made any attempt to get up. Relentless mall noise whirled around me from all directions, and time crawled forward in slow motion.

What relief I felt when Ian's voice came into the mix, and what a sense of gratitude that he had dropped everything to rescue me! I was unsure about my physical stability, so Ian stepped into a nearby store to ask for a plastic bag. After a few moments, I moved to get out of the chair.

How life's situations can change so quickly. One moment I'm a lady exiting an expensive salon; the next, I'm a crumpled heap in a chair, vomiting into a bag.

I can't go to Paris. How am I going to manage on my own for six days, when I can't even get home by myself from the mall?

Later, near midnight, with my headache well under control, we returned to the mall to retrieve my lonely car. We had no problem finding it on the deserted field of asphalt.

Most of the time, my migraines are manageable. It's rare to have such a rapid descent into the pain with nothing able to ease it. Deep down, I knew nothing could stop me from going to Paris. Nothing could hold me back from almost a full week on my own in the warm August sun, seeing whatever I chose, all at my own pace. Topping it off would be the most wonderful highlight: meeting up with my daughter, Hannah, and touring around Paris with her for another three days. The Eiffel Tower, the Louvre Museum, and Notre-Dame were on our list to explore together. This freed me up to visit some of the lesser known historical places in Paris on my own, so I threw myself into the research about places to seek out. Being on my own was usually not a problem, but I really didn't like the idea of being alone and ill. I brushed up on many French phrases, but I hadn't yet worked out, "Can you please help me? I think I'm going to be sick."

The next day, feeling tired but better, I went over my migraine medication with my doctor. It gave me a certain peace of mind and more confidence physically. Of course I could have thought back to my mother's old adage and taken some comfort in considering that, since my trip had the markings of a bad start, a great vacation awaited me—but I'm not superstitious so there was no comfort there.

Having been a Christian for more than thirty-five years, I knew that real comfort lay in knowing God would be with me at every step. Scripture verses came to my mind that promised God's presence. These were

3

promises meant to be claimed, meant to comfort, like Jesus' promise to be with us *"always, to the very end of the age"* (Matthew 28:20).

But I didn't feel comforted, despite my inner theological voice saying, "Of course, God is always with you. You're indwelt by the Holy Spirit." I desired a *special* sense of God's presence. I felt oddly insecure and wanted to feel assured that God would be with me in Paris, but that didn't happen.

I told myself to get a grip. My travels were not to a country torn apart by civil war. I didn't have to pack my mosquito net and malaria pills to join up with a tropical mission team. My path wasn't the sacrificial kind where one might think a Christian would require a special sense of God's presence.

What reassurances of God did the average tourist need? There was nothing heroic about the path of a person fully intent on sitting at outdoor cafes in Paris, visiting fine museums, buying a lovely scarf or two. I would be just another tourist like millions of others, with Euros, credit cards and a return ticket home.

I was fairly sure I wouldn't have another migraine episode, and I didn't believe that I would pass out on the banks of the Seine. But then I started to imagine myself passing out on the banks of the Seine. I also saw myself vomiting and collapsing on a park bench far away from my hotel. Being a short, slight-of-frame, middle-aged woman on iron supplements, I wondered if I'd even be noticed if I did collapse.

Then I realized the heart of the problem. I was assured about God's presence, in the sense that He would be somewhere in my vicinity. But even after so many years, I doubted that He would actually be close to me personally. I doubted His loving care for me. I doubted my importance to Him.

But I had to believe that God would be as close to me as He would be to any of His children, that God travels alongside the vacationer. He wouldn't dismiss me or forget about me while I went on a holiday where it appeared that I wouldn't be doing much spiritually, as if He would be back in touch with me upon my return. Blessings are not suspended until we're back to work, back to ministry, back to what some call real life. God is the God of all of our times, the God of all moments. He has met me in the darkest times of my life and I needed to believe He would be equally with me in the brightest times. He is the God of the good and the exciting, not only our pain and sorrow. I need such a God, because when fun opportunities come along in life, I want to enjoy them. I don't want fear, worry or guilt to dampen those joyful times.

Any reassurance I wanted had to be by faith, believing God saw me as important. I knew that wherever I went in the world, even if it was only across the street, desiring God's presence was okay. He promises His constant presence. And constantly is how often I need Him. I had to believe and start packing.

The next few days were busy ones, confirming my belief that getting ready for vacation is almost enough to warrant one. Then, while packing the afternoon before my flight, came an unexpected moment—a moment where I sensed the presence of God. It surprised me because I had become content with my faith alone, not seeking or even secretly desiring a feeling of God's presence. I had let that go.

I stood in my bedroom, packing my purse and one suitcase to go as carry-on luggage. Everything I was taking had to fit well and stay within the weight limit. I arranged and rearranged, over and over. My purse would be slung over my shoulder as I huffed it through the Amsterdam and Paris airports, and the Paris train and Métro stations. I aimed at having my purse be as light as possible, yet contain everything I wanted at my fingertips—something nearly impossible. I don't know how long I worked at this, but I know I far extended the packing time of the average person.

Nearing a peak of frustration, I paused and glanced over at my daily calendar by my bedside. I hadn't read my spiritual quote for that particular day. Now, in the late afternoon and filled with concerns, I read a quote written by Phillip Brooks, a nineteenth-century American clergyman: "I pray not for a lighter load but for a stronger back."

I stood still, absolutely stunned. God allows things to coincide for reasons we may or may not understand. From that particular moment, three things happened.

Firstly, I became greatly encouraged, sensing God's personal touch. I took away from that moment the message that I needed to keep going in

Kim Louise Clarke

faith with the strength already given me. Travelling will always require us to have faith, whether or not we sense His presence.

Secondly, I completed my packing without more fussing. *No matter how I pack, my purse will be heavy. I cannot allow myself to be a wimp. I will have to use the muscles God gave me.*

And finally, from that point on, I began a collection of observed moments connected with my trip. Moments when something happened. Moments when I experienced a clear emotion—whether it was amusement, embarrassment, fear, excitement or curiosity. It didn't matter how small the moment. It didn't even matter whether it was a moment when I had a clear sense of God being present. It only had to be a moment noticed enough to be recorded in my memory. These would be moments I could sort through, arranging them so that I gained a deeper understanding of God and of myself in the situation—all in the unforgettable context of Paris. These moments would become what I call my French collection.

Wherever I would venture in Paris, in its past or present, on aged cobblestone streets, sitting on park benches, or strolling sidewalks lined with chestnut trees, I anticipated being with God. I needed Him. I needed His strength, to keep a strong back, and to walk with Him.

Before leaving for Paris I turned to one of my favourite psalms, Psalm 139, reading slowly:

Where can I go from your Spirit? Where can I flee from your presence? If I go up to the heavens, you are there; if I make my bed in the depths, you are there. If I rise on the wings of the dawn, if I settle on the far side of the sea, even there your hand will guide me, your right hand will hold me fast.
—Psalm 139:7-10

These words reinforced the extent of God's presence. I was reminded that as His child, I could not be separated from Him.

Departure day came. We left for the Calgary International Airport, where I would leave to fly to France. I passed through airport security, glancing back and waving goodbye to Ian and our son Philip. I gathered my suitcase and purse. Wearing sandals revealing my bright bijou toenails, I excitedly continued on to the gate, into the adventure awaiting me.

I think I looked like many others there, a self-sufficient traveller. But that wasn't the case because I knew how quickly I could become an inert crumpled heap. I knew every breath I breathed to keep me upright was God-given. Arriving in the waiting area, I sat in an unoccupied row of seats, but I was not alone: God travelled by my side. His right hand would hold me up.

I slept very little during the eight-hour overnight flight to Amsterdam, where I changed flights, landing at Charles de Gaulle airport, 10:30 a.m. Paris time. Using a detailed map of the airport, I
took a few moments to wander through the busy terminals getting a sense
of where I would meet Hannah in six days. In France, I felt much closer
to Hannah who was then currently in nearby England, a little over two
hundred miles away.

Once I felt familiar enough to navigate my way around, I left to find
the train station. It wasn't far and my excitement rose, knowing that I was
only a forty-five minute train ride from the centre of Paris.

In the station, automatic vending machines dispensed train tickets.
Feeling courageous, I approached one, hoping it would be easy to understand how to buy a ticket. I thought that the nine years of French I had
taken in grade school would have to be of some use and that if I had any
strength in French at all, it would be in reading, but I could neither understand the instructions nor even locate a slot to insert a credit card. A bit
discouraged, I left to stand in line at the ticket office.

After buying my ticket, I then proceeded to the wrong platform,
where the trains go everywhere in France except Paris. The large automatic glass doors opened for me. I stood around with other passengers
waiting for a train, and saw them holding their tickets, each the size of a
Kraft Dinner™ box. As mine was only the size of a Chiclet™ box, I started
to perspire. The doors I had entered through appeared to be the only ones

in or out, and I had an awful feeling that they were one-way. I stepped toward them, hoping that surely the next step would be the magic one to cause them to open. Thankfully, a group approaching from the other side triggered the doors, and I dashed past them and back out.

At the ticket office once again, I received clarification about the correct platform and went off toward my next mistake. Before me stretched a lengthy row of ticket-reading admission gates, none of them busy at the time. Having travelled before, I felt confident with my general understanding of how they worked. I reached out to insert my tiny ticket into a machine slot, which I knew would suck it in, like a zealous vacuum cleaner. It would then be spat out of the slot on the other side, allowing the bar in front of me to rise, so I could step through and retrieve it. A voice from behind abruptly stopped me.

"Non, non, madame! Ici!"

I pulled back my hand just in time and looked behind me to see a young man, with dark curly hair, who was probably eighteen years old. He continued speaking, and from his hand gestures, I understood that I was on the wrong side of the machine, in front of the wrong bar, trying to enter on the right side instead of the left.

Had I inserted my ticket, the bar would have risen on the left side, leaving me no time to scoot around with my suitcase and get through before the bar dropped back down. No catastrophe to be sure, but another ticket would have to be purchased to raise another bar.

I said *"merci"* to the young man. In fact, being so thankful, I may have said, *"merci beaucoup!"* It seemed the longer I remained in the airport area trying to get out, the more fluent I was becoming.

Later, I thought about God's guidance. Did God have anything to do with that? Or was it just the kindness of a nice young man? I have often heard the verse quoted from Isaiah, *"Whether you turn to the right or to the left, your ears will hear a voice behind you, saying, 'This is the way; walk in it'"* (Isaiah 30:21). The verse came to mind immediately even though in Isaiah, the context is much different. Isaiah was not talking about the leaving of a place, but the leaving of a faith as the Israelites left their faith in God and put it in foreign nations and gods. They called on others for help rather than relying solely on God. God waited for them to turn back to Him. He wanted to speak to them, but the people had to be willing to listen. *"How gracious he will be when you cry for help! As soon as he hears, he will answer you"* (Isaiah 30:19). When the Israelites' hearts were right and when they could welcome God's voice, then they would hear God's direction of the way they were to walk.

Since my family and I had prayed for God to guide me on my way to Paris, I believed that I could take all the kindnesses of people, even the smallest gestures, as part of His guidance. In a new way I learned that God still wants to guide His people today, that He wants nothing better than to help them along their way. He waits for us to ask for His help and He responds sometimes through other people.

After hearing *"Non, non, madame! Ici!"* I inserted my ticket in the proper slot, walked past the raised barrier, down a flight of stairs, and veered left, directly onto a train waiting to take me into the city of Paris. The day and night of travel had taken its expected toll. My body and mind were exhausted. I sat down in the train, tired but happy. It seemed right to give God credit. It seemed wrong not to say, "Thank you, God, for getting me here."

chapter 3
Spiral Staircases

*E*arly in the afternoon I arrived at the Gare du Nord train/Métro station in Paris, part of the intricate steel and concrete network that provides an efficient connection for thousands of people each day. I transferred and arrived underground at the Luxembourg Métro station. Dim flights of stairs brought me up to the sunlight's glare on the busy boulevard and connecting streets. I was a bewildered prairie gopher popping up out of a hole far beyond familiar territory.

The woman at the nearby convenience store proved helpful. Following her directions, plus some guesswork as to which of the three intersecting streets she meant for me to cross, I somehow found my way to my hotel, a small miracle given its location on such a quiet, inconsequential street.

The small lobby presented a quiet sophistication and a lovely relaxed atmosphere with its subdued earth-toned walls and warm lighting that complemented the pottery and wicker. There was no need to speak in French to the polite man behind the desk, but I made an effort with the basics. A tiny elevator took me to my fourth-floor room. The room was very small but no smaller than I had expected. It was fully adequate and quaint, with two single beds, an ensuite bathroom, closet, desk, chair and TV. Until Hannah arrived, one bed would serve as a grand organizing table.

I opened the tall window to be greeted immediately by waist-high lines of iron rails branching out into fanciful curls. No balconies were provided, but the window gave me a view of bright green ivy climbing to the chimney-top of the four-storey white apartment building across the street, complete with its tidy little balconies. Looking directly down, I felt happy to watch activity at the hotel entrance doors. I could see farther down the quiet streets beyond and up to the bright sky over the tops of many old buildings.

I had planned to stay awake for seven or eight more hours to be in sync with Paris time and to combat jetlag. By then it would be early morning in Calgary, and I would use the hotel phone to call home, letting everyone know of my safe arrival. I had chosen not to bring my cell phone, feeling confident that I could manage such a short time without phone apps, GPS systems, and my favourite game of spider solitaire.

In the meantime, my intentions for the afternoon were to cut across the nearby Luxembourg Gardens, making a beeline to the historic church- es in the St. Germain-des-Prés area on the Left Bank. These were great intentions, but I had very little energy. I made myself hang up my clothes and lock a few items away in the room safe. Somehow, after that, I gained a second wind of renewed energy and excitement. Everything else could stay in the suitcase. I had to get outside.

One would think such giddiness indicated that this was my first time in Paris—rather than my third. But decades lay in between my vis- its, explaining my delight. Twenty years before, almost to the month, our European family vacation had included three days in Paris. Hannah had been with us then as well, although as she had been only eight months old, she could not look back on that time in Paris with fond memories. To have gone up the Eiffel Tower, been inside Notre-Dame Cathedral and toured through the Louvre with absolutely no recollection of any of it was bad enough. But then, Hannah had had to endure our many stories about those adventures for the next twenty years. It seemed almost criminal.

Now, two decades later, the perfect opportunity had come to Han- nah. Spending several weeks in England with friends would allow her the opportunity to zip over to Paris to make her own memories—the fact that she wanted to make them with me was a marvellous blessing.

I closed my hotel room door behind me. My Paris adventure was about to begin. Four flights of stairs would be a good way to warm up for my walk, so I decided to begin my vacation the right way by taking stairs whenever I could. Down the hallway, I pushed open the door to the stairwell. The fourth-floor door slowly closed behind me. The lighting became dim. I proceeded down anyway, surprised to find a narrow, spiral staircase.

I had yet to realize that narrow, worn, spiral stairs were everywhere in Paris, whether they had been built in the twelfth century or the twenty-first. Twenty years before, with Hannah in a stroller, we had avoided stairs and instead sought out elevators. This time, I had resolved to find exercise opportunities.

But as I circled down and around, the dim stairwell became darker and darker until I found myself in complete blackness. I eased away from the wall to clutch the railing. In the eerie darkness, I mumbled "what an idiot", directing the words at myself but also thinking of the hotel management. I have worked in the management of seniors' apartment buildings where darkened stairways were unacceptable and complete blackouts were unthinkable.

By the railing where I stood, the step sharply decreased to a point with hardly enough room for a toe-hold. Hugging the rail, I eased my way down, stretching out my leg at each step to gingerly slide my foot over and down in search of a secure place, all the while wondering if the third floor door would even open. Perhaps all the doors were locked from the inside and I'd never get out. My daughter would arrive in six days. Surely she would search until she found me. Life had been so good only moments ago.

At the third floor, I fumbled for the door handle. To my relief, the door opened! I'm not sure why—perhaps it was the jetlag—but despite the available elevator, I stubbornly stuck to the stairs. The open third-floor doorway gave me sufficient light to quickly skip down to the second floor and nearly to the first. Confident now, I felt for the door handle and stepped out into the mercifully empty lobby. No one saw this newly arrived hotel guest exit the stairway, looking as if she had just escaped the muggy catacombs. Across the lobby, opening one more door, I stepped out onto the streets of Paris.

Many other staircases, corridors, obscure paths and passageways lay ahead of me in the upcoming days. They would lead me to discover the treasures of historical Paris. The passageways themselves would no doubt

... .esting, but I sought to get beyond these to reach the greater historical treasures. I didn't want to be sidetracked from my goal.

In life, many things can hinder us, but we need to be determined to keep going through the passage to arrive at the treasure we intended to find.

In the Christian life, the treasure we seek is Christ. Paul clearly writes about his desire for the church to discover this treasure:

> ... that they may have the full riches of complete understanding, in order that they may know the mystery of God, namely, Christ, in whom are hidden all the treasures of wisdom and knowledge.
> —Colossians 2:2-3

Christ is discovered when people hear about Him, and put their faith in Him. Paul writes in Romans, "*Consequently, faith comes from hearing the message, and the message is heard through the word about Christ*" (Romans 10:17).

We travel into Bible passages to keep connected to Christ and to learn more and more about Him, since in Christ "*are hidden all the treasures of wisdom and knowledge*" (Colossians 2:3). Even if we know the importance of the Bible, we can open the pages, get into a passage and yet never arrive at the treasure of Jesus Christ. I don't come close to God if my heart is not open. The passage remains dark and I miss out.

I can also miss out on the treasure when I enter a familiar passage and quickly skim or skip over a particular portion because I've been down that Bible passage so many times before and I don't think I can learn anything new. But God's Word can never be exhausted. We'll never fathom the depth of every passage. If I am teachable, God will show me treasures of Himself I have yet to grasp.

I can miss out on the treasure when I enter Bible passages feeling smug about my daily Bible reading habits. I can be impressed with myself and my chart showing all the checkmarks in the little squares. Routine reading and checking can be great only if my heart is set upon seeking Christ, seeking to be impressed with Him.

I can miss out on the treasure when the passage becomes difficult. Confronted with things I don't like, reams of detail, lists of genealogies, difficult names or disturbing content, it is tempting to turn away in search of an easier passage. I'd prefer something like a short peaceful psalm. But the knowledge of Christ remains hidden until I venture in, prayerfully spending time and effort.

The Jewish leaders of Jesus' day travelled through the Scriptures backwards and forwards. Their knowledge of the Law was extensive as was their self-righteousness. They harassed Christ, trying to trap Him. They refused to see where the Scriptures were meant to lead them. They were definitely stuck, stuck in their heads with knowledge they refused to allow into their hearts. Jesus said of them:

> *You diligently study the Scriptures because you think that in them you possess eternal life. These are the very Scriptures that testify about me, yet you refuse to come to me to have life.*
> —John 5:39-40

Their hearts were not set on the true treasure of God—Jesus. They would prefer being stuck in a dark stairway instead of being out exploring the incredible treasures of Paris.

The Tuileries Garden and the Louvre

Walking in Gardens

"A garden to walk in and immensity to dream in—
what more could he ask?
A few flowers at his feet and above him the stars."
Victor Hugo, Les Misérables

"We can complain because rose bushes have thorns,
or rejoice because thorn bushes have roses."
Abraham Lincoln

"I cannot hear the orchestra of bird voices in my garden,
but the trees and flowers amaze me with their endless changes.
The pines drop pitch upon my hand,
and I know that summer is near."
Helen Keller

chapter 4

Crossing the Luxembourg

I stepped out of the lobby onto the street in the late afternoon sun with a clear plan. There were three sites I wanted to see in St. Germain-des-Prés; I could aim at a sensible return time near sunset.

I assumed my first stop would be at the Eglise St. Sulpice, situated not far beyond the other side of the Luxembourg Gardens. This large seventeenth-century Baroque church met with some damage during the turbulent years of the French Revolution in 1789-1799 when poverty ran rampant, religion was suppressed and the wealthy monarchy was despised. Restorations later took place in the nineteenth century, including the artistry of the Delacroix frescoes in its Chapel of the Angels.

Then I wanted to see the Eglise St. Germain-des-Prés, built in the sixth century, and which stands today as the oldest church in Paris. It endured the plundering of the Viking raiders. Centuries later it was used as a gunpowder magazine during the French Revolution. Today, it continues to function as a church building, steadfastly holding onto its original bell tower.

The third building I planned to visit was not as old as the churches: the Bon Marché department store was the first of its kind in Paris, and has operated continuously since 1852. I anticipated browsing among its fascinating upscale kitchen designer products and furnishings, and perhaps purchasing a lovely tea towel or potholder.

I entered the Luxembourg Gardens through tall wrought-iron gates to cut across the park and get to the churches. Passing a row of trees, the view opened in the direction I intended to cut across. I stopped abruptly.

I can't 'cut across' this. Cutting across this garden would have been like dull scissors carelessly ripping through a piece of finely spun silk. How could anyone, seeing sixty acres of green beauty stretching out in the distance, dotted with colourful flowerbeds and groves of trees (even palm trees!), do that? Placed all over the park were statues, a hundred and six of them. Some were perched high on columns; each one was a work of art. The crowning monument—the historic Luxembourg Palace—consumed the north end of the park.

And there were people everywhere! Some hung lazily around the huge central basin of sparkling water with its tall refreshing fountain in front of the Palace. Others reclined in chairs spread out everywhere in the sun, and just as many took up places in the shade under the trees.

Four hundred years of continued careful maintenance had passed since Queen Marie de Medici, widow of King Henry IV, had designed the gardens in 1612, influenced by her Italian background. I don't think she would have approved of a twenty-first-century tourist tearing across to get to the other side. This kind of beauty called for strolling, with camera in hand, and so that is what I did.

Two hundred years after the queen had established the gardens, they were expanded and took on a French formal look. At the far south end, six perfect rows of finely trimmed tall trees loomed up like giant green Popsicles in a gigantic hedge at least ten times my height.

They intrigued me enough to consider changing my plans. Why not drift down that way and loiter around the rows? How fascinating it might be to stand beneath them, gazing up at them, and taking fascinating angled photos. I felt like Alice in Wonderland (something I could also perhaps blame on jetlag).

Then the moment hit me: Paris was too big, not so much geographically, but too vast in terms of its beauty, history, culture and excitement. There was too much rich ground to cover in nine days. I felt like I had entered a race and I didn't know which way to run—or stroll. My vacation had merely started and already I felt pressed on all sides. Should I stop and see Popsicle hedges or hurry toward Viking marauders and designer tea towels? My indecision at all the excitement of Paris had me wasting precious seconds.

Anxiety began to do its work. Little nagging thoughts sprang up. *I probably won't get to see half of the places I want to. I'll probably reflect back on my trip and wonder what I was thinking. Why did I go here and didn't even go there? I didn't know this park was so big, with all these things to see. Why didn't I know this park was so big?*

When I think of anxiety, I picture a highlighter, anxious in itself but eager and evil too. It can hardly wait to pounce upon a thought, coat it a brilliant neon, and drag it forward to glow at the front of our minds.

If we allow it, anxiety will grow ever stronger. Anxiety wants to grow so strong that our muscles become tense and our hearts race. Anxiety wants to affect us to the point that we make bad choices and do foolish things.

The key in dealing with anxiety can be found in Philippians 4:5-7:

Let your gentleness be evident to all. The Lord is near. Do not be anxious about anything, but in every situation, by prayer and petition, with thanksgiving, present your requests to God. And the peace of God, which transcends all understanding, will guard your hearts and your minds in Christ Jesus.

Anxiety wants no share with gentleness. These two do not mix. Gentleness is possible when we understand how near God is to us. Gentleness, prayer, thanksgiving—these blend well together and lead to experiencing God's peace.

There in the garden, I had to catch myself from giving in to anxiety. I no more wanted my time to be a constant race around Paris than I wanted to spend six days in a park looking up at trees. The decisions were mine to make. I could make them with anxiety or I could relax with God and make them in gentleness, thanksgiving and prayer.

I decided to carry on toward the exit of the Luxembourg Gardens, and began making my way toward Rue Bonaparte. When I found the street, I realized I had already passed the Eglise St. Sulpice so I carried on toward Eglise St. Germain-des-Prés. This small, white church was adorned with colourful flowers in window boxes. The doors were locked and I couldn't see inside the oldest church in Paris so I enjoyed seeing what I could of its surroundings.

In searching for the location of the Bon Marché department store, I interrupted a woman's meaningful walk to ask for directions. The conversation didn't go well. I repeated my words with slow deliberation while fighting my inner voice that said, "You are lousy at speaking French, and you have a terrible accent."

But just then her face brightened. "Ah, Bon Marché!" she said, and pointed me in the right direction.

The merchandise in this historic department store was as beautifully displayed as an art gallery, a combination of high fashion, home furnishings and fabulous foods. The female employees clad in severe navy suits manned their departments like stern guards, creating a 'look but don't under any circumstances touch' atmosphere. Despite their gazes, it was fun to browse. Eventually, I spotted small bundles of quilting fabric known as 'fat quarters' on a sales table and, after choosing a couple of them, proceeded to the cashier.

The cashier, clearly unhappy about being disturbed, offered me her coldest, most stony stare. Somehow, she resisted calling Maintenance to have me swept out of the store, and reluctantly proceeded with my unimpressive purchase. I inched away from the area, stunned at having been treated in such a way, and yet proud that I still had the wherewithal to tuck the receipt into my wallet.

I had entered the store at five-foot-three tall, and stubbornly decided that I wasn't about to leave feeling only an inch high. I knew a café existed on one of the floors. When I found it, I ordered a black decaf coffee and dessert, and settled myself at a table overlooking the street. Expecting a big mug of coffee, I still smiled at the pleasant waiter when he brought me the tiniest espresso. I savoured all three sips, and thoroughly enjoyed the delicious pistachio macaron.

I practiced being anxious about nothing and I made it a point to enjoy the moments. *"Let your gentleness be evident to all."* Even to those who wear navy blue suits, and live lives I know nothing about. Gentleness and peace.

Nothing of the busy street below my window attracted my attention, so my thoughts roamed widely. They sailed prayerfully across the ocean to my family. They reflected upon the past twenty hours of travel. They settled upon the here and now, and I felt blessed to be on this adventure.

I left the Bon Marché still liking the store, unaware that the route I chose would position me to encounter the Eglise St. Sulpice with no effort on my part. The doors were wide open for visitors, so I walked with fascination down the long corridors of this seventeenth-century church with its vaulted ceilings and frescoes. I couldn't leave without taking photos of the large fountain outside which was guarded by fierce marble lion statues.

The early evening sky was filled with light, and the air still held a wonderful warmth. My leisurely walk back to my hotel brought me to a northerly entry of the Luxembourg Gardens. I thought about the tall hedge-like trees looming row on row at the south end, but thoughts of my hotel room and sleep towered higher than hedges.

A path led toward the grand Luxembourg Palace. It grew into a pebbled walkway bordered with stunning red geraniums. I kept walking in the early evening shadows, along a gorgeous scarlet trail of geraniums that collided with the stonework of the seventeenth-century palace. Once across the Luxembourg Gardens and past several more streets, I spotted the entrance doors to my hotel. The elevator would do fine. It had been a wonderful first day in Paris.

chapter 5
Trouble in the Tuileries

ach morning, with a tentative plan in mind, I left my hotel room to head toward a museum, a monument, a church or some structure of old. Most often I would head north, and a fifteen-minute walk would bring me to the Seine River, dividing the Left Bank from the Right Bank. Twenty-three bridges cross the Seine River in the city of Paris alone.

My favourite route took me across the Seine at Île de la Cité, a small island where Paris first began and which is utterly dominated by the magnificence of Notre-Dame Cathedral. A three- to four-kilometre radius of museums, churches and gardens grew out from Île de la Cité.

On the Right Bank I walked parallel with the Seine, admiring the calm waters and tour boats. Then I glanced across the street to the architecture of the Louvre's Denon wing. Whichever way you look, the vistas of Paris are enchanting.

Past the Louvre lies another famous French garden, the Tuileries. Close to half a kilometre long, the Tuileries Garden stretches all the way from the grounds of the Louvre to the Place de la Concorde. 'Tuile' is French for tile, and the name of the gardens comes from the tiles once manufactured from the local clay and used to roof many of the surrounding buildings.

The Tuileries Garden was designed in 1564 for another Italian-born Queen of France, Catherine de Medici. A hundred years later, French landscape gardener André Le Nôtre brought more formality to the garden for King Louis XIV. When the King's court moved to Versailles in 1682, the

Tuileries Garden was left in all its beauty to become a stylish place for elegant Parisians—it was the place where one would want to be seen. After the French Revolution, it became a public park for every citizen to enjoy.

Impressionist artists like Camille Pissarro, Edward Manet and Pierre-Auguste Renoir often set up their canvases and easels in the Tuileries, to capture its beauty. It certainly fit in with Renoir's personal vision and purpose of his art: "Why shouldn't art be pretty? There are enough unpleasant things in the world."

Today, it remains a garden for the masses, offering many paths to stroll and places to sit. But one morning, the beauty and serenity of the garden faded for me. I had stopped to take a photograph and overheard a few words between a mother and teenage daughter. They appeared to be talking about finances. The mother asked a question to which the daughter calmly replied that she had spent the money. The body language and facial contortions of the mother warned me of imminent eruption. Angry words flew back and forth. The daughter stomped off in a fury toward the site of the guillotines of old. The mother panicked, realizing that she had lost control of the situation, and followed frantically after her daughter.

For that brief moment, the three of us failed to see anything beautiful in the garden. The anger expressed by the mother, felt by her daughter and observed by me destroyed the serenity of the landscape. My eyes followed the mother and daughter until they blended into the crowd, leaving me to wonder how things would turn out for them. Like getting back to a lovely meal after experiencing nasty heartburn, I attempted to find again the beauty of the garden.

I took a few more photographs and continued farther down the park, where the tall form of the ancient Egyptian *Obelisk of Luxor* marked the centre of the distant Place de la Concorde. The obelisk, a gift to France from the Ottoman ruler of Egypt, was erected in Place de la Concorde by King Louis Phillippe in the 1830s in honour of Louis XVI and his wife, Marie Antoinette. It stands in the very place where they and twelve hundred others, were guillotined during the French Revolution.

Just before the Place de la Concorde, there is a small museum, the Musée de l'Orangerie. On the lawn outside this museum stand several life-sized statues. One of them is Auguste Rodin's 1899 fascinating portrayal

24

of Eve. Like the mother and her daughter I saw, the statue shows th; too, no longer enjoys the garden. This Eve has definitely bitten into the fruit. She stands with her right arm wrapped around her chest, trying to hide her nakedness. Her head is down and her left hand shields her face, palm outward. I stared at Eve for a moment, feeling sorry for this figure in great anguish, hiding her face from God. "Please, don't look at me".

But God always looks and always sees. There is no hiding from Him. *"For your ways are in full view of the Lord, and he examines all your paths"* (Proverbs 5:21).

He looks because He loves. Our tangled messes matter to God. He doesn't abandon us in the gardens that we spoil. God didn't leave the garden and abandon Adam and Eve after they sinned. *"Then the man and his wife heard the sound of the Lord God as he was walking in the garden in the cool of the day"* (Genesis 3:8).

God knows that it doesn't take us long to mess up our walk in the park. He knows how easily we wreck the most beautiful places of the earth. Even the most beautiful places with lovely ambiance, surrounded in tranquility have nothing magical within them that can help us behave any better there than anywhere else. We still remain sinners and need help. Only God can provide what we need.

The only beauty that has any power over sin is the beauty of the Lord and what He did about our sin. Getting angry, running off, hiding our faces—these things do not benefit us when what we need is forgiveness. We can bring every difficult situation to God and receive His help. In Christ, God has provided everything we need. *"In him we have redemption through his blood, the forgiveness of sins, in accordance with the riches of God's grace that he lavished on us"* (Ephesians 1:7-8).

O nce a greenhouse for orange trees, the Musée de l'Orangerie stands at the west end of the Tuileries. Today it is a museum of Impressionist and Post-Impressionist art. Inside the museum I sat and was completely surrounded by Monet's water lilies curving around the entire room, dusk following dawn in magnificent, serene beauty. He wrote, "I am following nature without being able to grasp her. Nature won't be summoned to order and won't be kept waiting. It must be caught, well caught."

After peaceful moments considering the lilies, I left l'Orangerie to lean against an ornate concrete wall and to survey the view below. People dawdled and the waters bubbled at the two fountains at Place de la Concorde. The Fontaine des Fleuves and the Fontaine des Mers were designed to commemorate France's trade and navigation upon the rivers and oceans. The Place de la Concorde was designed as an octagon, with a statue at each point to represent eight cities of France. Beyond, I could see the beginnings of the Champs-Élysées. In the far distance stood the unmistakable form of the Arc de Triomphe.

To my left, also in the distance—there it stood. For the first time in Paris this trip, I caught sight of the Eiffel Tower. That moment's excitement contained tinges of dread because before coming to Paris, I had discovered that the Eiffel Tower had been experiencing elevator difficulties. Lineups for tickets to the functioning lifts were exceedingly long. To make matters worse, tickets could no longer be purchased online. One could stand in line for a long time.

On the other hand, visitors could take the stairs up to the first and second levels. Since I had already been up the Eiffel Tower, I didn't need to pursue that experience. But I knew how much Hannah wanted to go up the Eiffel Tower. We had determined that if we had to wait forever for an elevator, we could at least take the stairs. We wouldn't get to the top but it was a reasonable option.

Now as I peered out at the tower, so distant and yet incredibly tall, I wondered if perhaps the six-thousand miles of land and ocean between us at the time had hampered my good judgment. To climb 704 steps on outside open metal stairs was plain foolish. My hands get clammy just crossing pedestrian overpasses. What was I thinking? How embarrassing would it be if I had to be rescued, a fear-frozen tourist on the Eiffel Tower stairs? I decided that Hannah and I would figure things out when we arrived at the tower. In the meantime, I would not check on the elevator status.

Back in Calgary, where brave thoughts came more easily, I had attempted to get in better physical shape in case I did have to climb the stairs. I had started with brisk walks. Then I advanced to a descent of the wooden stairs from McHugh's Bluff above the Bow River down toward Prince's Island Park. Then I'd stroll over to Eau Claire Market for a coffee break in preparation for the grueling ascent back up the 166 steps. It was nowhere near the number needed to reach the second floor of the Eiffel Tower, but it was something.

The more I had read about Paris, the more I had seen the need to be in better physical shape. Notre-Dame contained stairs, as did the Arc de Triomphe, not to mention the miles we would accumulate along the streets and inside museums. Despite my motivation, none of my exercise efforts came easily after not keeping up with any exercise routine for several years.

Even though Paul wrote that *"physical training is of some value"* (I Timothy 4:8), I had easily excused myself from exercising, primarily perhaps because he said it amounted only to *some* value, sliding past those first words of the verse because the next ones are so significant: *"but godliness has value for all things, holding promise for both the present life and the life to come."*

I seemed to have convinced myself that the word 'some' in the original Greek meant 'none, zero, nil'. But it doesn't. The Greek word translated 'some' is 'ŏligŏs' meaning 'a little, few, a season, a while'. There is definitely some value in physical exercise for my present life here.

The difficulty was that I simply didn't like to exercise. I didn't like getting out of breath, knowing that the next breath would be more difficult and the next one after that even more so. I didn't like feeling that I couldn't go on.

Physical education had been my worst subject in school, right from the start. All the other subjects in elementary school came easily to me, including math and even French. But I couldn't figure out why everyone else ran laps so easily, and did push-ups and sit-ups without much complaint. I would tire immediately and often ended up with headaches.

Our family doctor had found nothing wrong with me. Every checkup and test showed that I was healthy. Second medical opinions were not commonly sought back in the 1960s. Gradually my headaches and fatigue worsened. For me, a small hill had to be trudged, and a little jaunt became a journey. I always lagged behind everyone else.

With my growing distress, the doctor finally referred me to a specialist. It wasn't long before the cardiologist discovered the problem, and immediately scheduled me for open-heart surgery for a congenital atrial septal defect to repair a hole in my heart. At fourteen years old, and about to enter grade nine, I had to miss the first month of school but the successful surgery improved my health immediately with rich oxygenated blood nourishing my entire system for the first time in my life.

God graciously guided me through my heart repair without subsequent complications. Today, if I don't keep up with some kind of cardio exercise I can begin to feel as if I am fourteen years old all over again. And that is a scary feeling. I firmly believe that God expects me to take care of myself physically, as long as I have the capacity.

So I have no excuse, even though I still don't like to exercise. I have always loved this passage:

From heaven the Lord looks down and sees all mankind; from his dwelling place he watches all who live on earth—he who forms the hearts of all, who considers everything they do.

—Psalm 33:13-15

There may be physical limits and weaknesses that legitimize our reasons for not doing things, but more often than not, we tend to manufacture excuses. Excuses are powerful deterrents in our lives. Although they are mere words or thoughts, they can bind us so tightly that it becomes very difficult just to get up off the couch.

*Some*how we must accommodate room in life to do *some*thing, because, as Paul maintains, there is *some* value in physical exercise.

*D*id he hesitate for a second? It was so slight, but I'm fairly sure that the waiter, well-dressed in black trousers and white shirt, gave a moment's pause and glanced down when taking my menu. What could have distracted him for that brief moment?

As soon as the waiter left, I peeked down. The café table hid my legs. Nothing showed except for my right foot. A fine light gray dust coated my foot entirely, and the red leather of my sandal had suddenly aged to a weather-beaten rust. The leather didn't quite cover a bandage, my attempt to deal with an oncoming blister. No shine could be seen in the muted colour of my nail polish. No wonder he had hesitated. It probably did not help that, along with my lunch order, I had made a point of asking for water. The waiter's professionalism likely had prevented him from giving into curiosity, but I'm sure he wanted to know what desert I had just trekked across.

I untwisted my legs, tucking both feet under my chair, out of sight of staff and patrons. Nonchalantly, I glanced at other women's feet—their perfect, immaculately sandaled feet which needed no hiding. Would any of them believe that only days ago I had glowed radiantly from head to toe, at least for a moment, stepping out of an expensive salon?

Before arriving at the café, I had explored the entire length of the Tuileries from the Louvre to the Place de la Concorde. A wide stretch of pavement running down the centre allows room for the crowd to stroll great lengths of the park but it stands wide open to the sun. Many, including me, chose to travel a shaded parallel path instead, beneath the chestnut and elm trees where its asphalt has broken down into fine powdery dust.

I wondered about all those other people who had walked the asphalt path with me. Where did they stop for lunch? What cafés were they sitting in? Or had the fine dust somehow not clung to them?

I was amazed how dreadful my feet looked. I could have gone to the washroom to tidy them up but it would mean leaving my table and exposing my feet.

It really was best to stay put and enjoy lunch. I never waited long for my meals anyway, possibly because I didn't order anything complicated. Nothing bordered on the exotic, nor would it until Hannah arrived. Hannah, who was fluent in French after thirteen years of immersion schooling and international language accreditation, could easily advise me on complex menu items. Meanwhile, 'chicken' and 'ham' were easy words to recognize and pronounce in French. I managed well, ordering *poulet* or *jambon* sandwiches, crepes and salads. When I didn't want chicken or ham, a simple pizza would suffice. None of the meals I ordered ever disappointed me. Fantastic food abounded everywhere.

My lunch arrived and I soon forgot about my feet. I enjoyed the meal, the café and the ambiance. Afterwards, I stepped out of the café, to find a nearby bench. Always having ample Kleenex™ in my purse, I tidied up my feet and sandals as best as I could, which improved their appearance considerably. I carried on with my day, looking forward to my evening shower.

It had been an embarrassing moment, although perhaps only the waiter and I noticed. How easy for my feet to get dusty and dirty since I walked every day in many parks. Obviously, I needed to observe my feet more often, and to take better care. I wasn't going to avoid the parks and gardens: they were great places of beauty where I sat, rested, wrote and watched life.

It was unfortunate that these parks and gardens were not similar to some beaches I know where outdoor public showers for rinsing off your sandy feet are available. I felt it was too bad that the social custom of foot washing is no longer practiced. That practice goes far back, at least to the times of Abraham who brought water for his visiting guests to wash their feet before they ate (Genesis 18:4). That practice carried forward into the New Testament times but not into our culture.

In embarrassing moments, I try to remember that people tend to notice us less than we think. They are occupied with their own lives, rather than taking note of strangers. I try to maintain perspective, correct what can be corrected, and remind myself that I will survive the moment.

Embarrassing moments are also easier to manage when a friend is there to help you through them. I knew I wasn't alone at the café table since God is always present. I took some comfort when I remembered that God understood this situation quite well. Jesus found Himself in a moment when He was about to eat a meal, but His feet were covered with the dirt of the paths He had travelled that day. *"When one of the Pharisees invited Jesus to have dinner with him, he went to the Pharisee's house and reclined at the table"* (Luke 7:36) without being offered a way to wash his feet. Jesus said to the Pharisee, *"I came into your house. You did not give me any water for my feet…"* (Luke 7: 44).

The Pharisee did not show the customary respect toward Jesus. As it turned out, though, Jesus's feet *were* washed:

> *A woman in that town who lived a sinful life learned that Jesus was eating at the Pharisee's house, so she came there with an alabaster jar of perfume. As she stood behind him at his feet weeping, she began to wet his feet with her tears. Then she wiped them with her hair, kissed them and poured perfume on them.*
> —Luke 7:37-38

Unlike the Pharisee, she knew that, as a sinner, her place belonged at the feet of Christ. She worshipped Jesus as Lord, and Jesus told her that her sins had been forgiven.

Later, when the time drew close to the Passover Feast, Christ astonished His disciples. *"He poured water into a basin and began to wash his disciples' feet"* (John 13:5). The disciples, who had watched as Christ was worshipped by the woman as she anointed His feet with perfume, now had their own feet washed by Jesus. With Christ, everyday practices become full of meaning. Consequently, we are daily reminded of Christ's lessons.

The disciples believed Jesus was the Lord, the One to be worshipped, the One they were to follow. Jesus said, *"I have set you an example that you should do as I have done for you. Very truly I tell you, no servant is greater than his master"* (John 13:15-16). After Jesus washed the disciples' feet, their feet would become dirty again, but the lessons they learned made a lasting impact on them.

Those lessons reach us today. Christ, our Master, expects us to humbly serve one another. Like the washing of feet, the serving of other people is a humble and an ongoing service. It is to be an ongoing daily practice. It's to be our lifestyle.

chapter 8

Daisies and Billy Goats

*T*he beauty of the colourful flowerbeds draws the tourist in, inviting us to meander around the quiet courtyard garden of the Palais Royal. We stroll the cool, shady paths between rows of lime trees, and congregate near the lovely fountain spray that shimmers in the sunshine. I didn't need to be drawn in: this walk around the Royal Palace gardens, designed back in 1630, was already on my list.

The Royal Palace, completed in 1639, served at first as the residence of Cardinal Richelieu, only later becoming the property of King Louis XIII. The history of the building is rich with kings and queens, theatre and art. Today, as an elegant series of apartments, the inner suites give view to the beauty of the historic gardens below. On the ground floor, shops, boutiques and restaurants open up with entries at the garden level.

I noticed waiters preparing for the lunch crowds, giving attention to the café tables outside. Each small round table became smartly dressed with a richly coloured linen, topped with a single flower in a vase. Ornate but petite chairs were tucked under the tables, and everything was set in tight, straight rows, much like the gardens themselves. With a professional touch, the outdoor restaurants had been thoughtfully prepared and planted, taking full advantage of the view to the gardens.

The flowers, plants, and hedges, trimmed to perfection, provided pleasing eye-level views for those lifting forks to their mouths, or wine glasses to their lips. Shrubs, rose bushes and tall flowering plants were kept in line so as not to annoy those sitting on park benches.

The plants, kept within their beds of rich soil, performed th
tions well. When I stood near the flowers, it seemed to me that their main
function was to serve as borders and frames. They drew attention to something more important than themselves—the statues.

One such statue in the Royal Garden was a work of marble done by
Paul Lemoyne in 1830. It's entitled *La Pâtre et la Chèvre*—The Shepherd
and the Goat. The shepherd wrestles with the goat at his hip. With his
arm around the goat's head, the shepherd tries to direct the goat to turn
around to follow him. It looks like a bit of a battle. Who is the stronger?
This story carved in marble draws attention at the place where tourists
stop to take photos.

The flowers get included in the picture by default because they add
nicely to the foreground or background. Unless a flower contest is under-
way, who would concentrate on one particular flower? The pink roses are
beautiful, but each one has bloomed exactly like the one beside it. The
purple spikey flowers all appear to be the same. The daisy-type flowers
look like all the other daisy-types. There doesn't seem to be any difference between them. But if you were a flower, that's not what you would
want to hear.

I was a daisy kind of flower once. There on a hillside, I stood surrounded by other daisies. The huge paper petals around my face, I believe,
were orange. My role as a flower for our grade three performance of The
Three Billy Goats Gruff required me to stand and smile.

During the 1960s, the average class size was thirty. We needed three
billy goats and one troll. We may have had a narrator. So when I do the
math, there were no clear roles for twenty-five students. What does a
teacher do with these extra students? You send them across the bridge to
the beckoning hillside so they can stand as smiling flowers.

In this Norwegian story, there are three billy-goat brothers who need
to cross a bridge to eat the grass on the other side. However, a terrible troll
lives under the bridge, and will eat anyone travelling across. The smallest
goat goes over first, convincing the troll to let him cross and wait for his
older brother who is bigger and better to eat. The second goat does likewise. When the third and biggest goat arrives, the troll is no match for

the goat with such big horns. The billy goat easily pushes the troll off the bridge and the troll is never seen again.

Perhaps the moral of the story we learned in grade three was that not all of us could be billy goats, the ones receiving most of the attention from the audience. The goats gave voice and action to the story. The parents of the flowers would search the hillside for our familiar faces, but then, we knew, their focus would shift to the action.

However, we also learned in grade three that everyone must be involved. The teachers made sure of it. Everyone needed a costume of sorts because everyone had to be visible on stage with a role to play. Content with being a flower, I performed my part well, even without attention. As a group, we flowers showed our importance by enhancing the stage set. I only envied the goats a little bit because I was not jealous of all the pressure their roles placed upon them. And yet, the goats carried out their parts well, with complete ease, as if the pressure didn't bother them at all.

The picture here in the Royal Garden was similar. Like the children dressed as goats, or the marble goat in the garden, goats seemed to be the stars of the show. But don't mistake the importance of the flowers. The dull grey sculptures were not as spectacular from a distance. Were it not for the brilliant flowers, some would never even venture into the courtyard to begin with. The views while dining would go unappreciated. Even Monet credited them with his career when he wrote: "I perhaps owe having become a painter to flowers." So the flowers also have stories to tell.

In a garden or a skit, each part is important and has great value. Each has a role to play, as we all do in life, exactly where God has placed us. God has gifted us and knows where we fit best in life's ministries. He will lead us to those places. *"But in fact God has placed the parts in the body, every one of them, just as he wanted them to be"* (I Corinthians 12:18).

God cares for His body—the Church—wanting it to grow and mature. Each person is unique and valued by God. Each Christian should know and treasure their own story. Each has their personal story about Christ to share with the world, to be shared in the ways they have been gifted. Anything to do with revealing Christ, anytime we seek to do something for His glory—that's where God wants us.

Being the Church is not about standing around on a hillside smiling, nor is it a constant grueling battle with trolls. Whether on a large stage before thousands of people or behind the scenes doesn't matter. To God, I believe we are all centre stage. Our lives are a calling to work together with all others in the body to be effective in the world through the power of the Holy Spirit.

The Royal Garden was developed four hundred years ago from a design. Nothing is there by accident, but it is planned, maintained, weeded and pruned season after season. Everything is in its place and it works well.

*I*n Paris, a tourist simply walking around the city can see almost a thousand sculptures. Collectively these represent the art of more than four hundred sculptors, whose works have become permanent art fixtures in gardens and streets, and on building and monument façades. It makes walking around the city an amazing experience. But after a few days, like museum fatigue, statue fatigue can set in.

In the Royal Palace Gardens, I noticed the Shepherd and the Goat statue because it struck me as an interesting story, but there was a second statue—one I didn't study very long. As I took my obligatory photo of the statue of this young man sitting with his arms raised chest level, a bird momentarily perched itself upon the statue's head. The bird's profile showed prominently in my photo, enough to destroy any artistic impression. But my bird-interrupted photo had to suffice. Although it was not yet noon, statue fatigue had already hit. Perhaps from watching the waiters set up their café tables, I began thinking about crepes. For several days, I had noticed them listed in café menus but had yet to bite into one. So I left the Royal Palace Gardens to remedy that.

That second marble statue, the one I paused at so briefly, had been created by Adolphe Thabard in 1875. It startled me later when I discovered the name of the statue: *Le Charmeur du Serpent*—The Snake Charmer.

What snake? There had been no snake.

The sculptured youth sits with arms raised and face looking down, with a slight grin, toward where his left hand would have been—but his left hand has been broken off along with the entire snake. Many images of the statue indicate that the snake has been missing for several years.

It is not too difficult to imagine what role a snake in the garden would represent. And a missing snake would be a very ominous thing indeed. A clever snake hiding somewhere in the garden never hides for long, and seeks to strike the unguarded. Likewise, Satan prepares himself, seeking out his next victim, ready to tempt, ready to attack.

Like the snake, the devil is not easily detected. He's tricky that way. Especially when we are fatigued in our faith, growing lax in spiritual awareness. That's when we don't sense anything false. Everything is absolutely fine according to our spiritually sleepy minds. We begin to accept things that are not right, as if over time God's Word has changed. The devil can be so subtle that we can live day after day forgetting we even have an enemy.

Paul speaks about false apostles:

For such people are false apostles, deceitful workers, masquerading as apostles of Christ. And no wonder, for Satan himself masquerades as an angel of light. It is not surprising, then, if his servants masquerade as servants of righteousness.

—II Corinthians 11:13-15

The church can become as dull as a butter knife instead of as sharp as a sword if we become lazy in reading, studying and applying the Word of God. We need to keep ourselves sharp in the knowledge of Christ. Paul uses an animal analogy to warn us about Satan and our need to be aware. *"Be alert and of sober mind. Your enemy the devil prowls around like a roaring lion looking for someone to devour"* (I Peter 5:8).

Despite my statue fatigue, my stroll around the Royal Palace gardens had been pleasant. I left and stepped onto the busy streets nearby. It was such a difference from the tranquil gardens to the action-packed scenes of streets and crowds. At a crowded restaurant, I was led to a table squeezed in among many, where I enjoyed a delicious chicken and mushroom crepe, and a refreshing tall glass of water. It was a leisurely break, and

39

being physically rested, I set out to explore again. I distanced myself from the gardens, blissfully unaware of the missing snake. Thankfully it was only one made of marble.

A street in the Latin Quarter

All in a Day

"The secret of your future
is hidden in your daily routine."
Mike Murdock

"The best things in life are nearest:
Breath in your nostrils, light in your eyes, flowers at your feet,
duties at your hand, the path of right just before you.
Then do not grasp at the stars,
but do life's plain, common work as it comes,
certain that daily duties and daily bread
are the sweetest things in life."
Robert Louis Stevenson

"The things you take for granted,
someone else is praying for."
Author Unknown

he sun had set and the arched bridges over the Seine River were silhouetted against a soft pink skyline. I made my way slowly through the lively Latin Quarter, stopping for dinner and to browse at boutiques. A few days had now passed and I felt comfortable in Paris, taking my time returning to my hotel in the early evenings.

Back at my hotel room, I developed a nightly routine: shower, watch the world news on TV, write in my journal and read. I always travel with a good book, usually a mystery. But a frustration in Paris grew because although I had brought a mystery book, it was not a good one.

In my pile of unread mysteries at home, I had chosen one to pack for my vacation. I didn't choose it because it had the best cover. Worse than that, I chose it because it was thin and lightweight. Unbeknownst to me, the author had determined that the protagonist (naturally the main detective privileged with the most dialogue) would swear in almost every sentence.

Not every book that comes across my path needs to be read and after a few days, I decided not to persist any longer with this one. It became imperative to seek out a replacement mystery written by a familiar and trusted author. I knew exactly where I needed to go in Paris to do so. I now had two quests before me for the next morning.

My other quest was one I had recognized as a necessity the very first time I entered my hotel room. The lack of a coffee maker in my room always had me out of my hotel each morning around 7:30. Paris is quiet at that time of day with only a handful of people outside, most of whom are striding off to work.

In the mornings, I would exit the hotel main doors, ready to be embraced by the early morning warmth, knowing that I could get away without wearing layers. Layers are a year-round way of life in Calgary situated as it is so close to the Rocky Mountains, but I could toss that aside while in Paris in August. I could leave my light jacket or sweater back in my room. To wear capris or a skirt with summer top and sandals proved sufficient from morning until well after sunset.

A French *boulangerie* not far from my hotel became my favourite place for breakfast. The constant fresh smell of ground coffee wafted up from behind the counter. Each morning, enticing fruit-filled croissants and other fresh baked goods lay pleasantly arranged under the curved Plexiglas. But on the morning of my added quest for a mystery novel, I arrived too early. The bakery had yet to open.

The restaurant next door—McDonald's—was open for business but sat almost empty. In fact, it always seemed to be open. But wasn't entering the doors of a McDonald's akin to a character weakness, almost like admitting I needed a coffee break from the French culture? Shouldn't tourists do their utmost to completely immerse themselves in the culture they visit? I wasn't tired of French culture but my coffee desire was too strong to resist. Opening those doors and entering a McDonald's zapped me through a portal, sending me back into my own culture and my neighbourhood where I really didn't want to be. I wanted to remain in France and so to assuage my guilt, I attempted to converse with the employees in French, despite their ability and willingness to serve me in English.

It didn't take long before entering a McDonald's restaurant became a strategic part of my vacation. This strategy hung upon a unique map that I had kept from my Paris trip twenty years before. It's a wonderfully detailed map, which I fast realized was the best of all three maps I possessed. Its uniqueness lay in the fact that it had originated from a McDonald's restaurant, and so it showed Paris dotted with little yellow Ms encased in red squares. I always knew the location of the closest McDonald's restaurant, throughout each day's journeys and subsequently discovered many new locations constructed over the past two decades. On any given day, when not hungry enough for a big meal or not ready for a leisurely break at a café, I knew that I could enter a McDonald's restaurant and confidently occupy a table for ten or fifteen minutes to rest my feet, having purchased only a coffee. I saved money by avoiding unnecessary food purchases, and I knew exactly where I could stop to fill up my water bottle, and use the washroom. It worked well.

That particular early morning, I stepped inside the doors of McDonald's, ordered a coffee and muffin, and found a table. The muffin tasted okay, but could hardly compare to what the fabulous *boulangerie* next door could offer. Keeping to myself, I sat drinking my coffee, my hands wrapped around the cup. This was my habit, holding not so tightly as to burn my hands, but skillfully, to maintain a comfortable and maximum warmth, as if I would soon be back outside enduring the winter's bitter cold.

I failed to notice him at first. He came into McDonald's and directly over to my table. This was hardly a surprise, since I was the only one sitting on that side of the restaurant. Apparently he asked if I had any money to give him, but his French words flew too rapidly for me to grasp even one of them. I looked up at him, offering no words in return. I searched his face to detect a clue as to what he was saying. Was he seeking directions? No, he didn't appear to be a tourist. Was he a regular customer, a creature of habit, and had I sat in his spot? Did I happen to be doing something wrong, sitting there with my muffin and small black coffee, wondering if large coffees existed anywhere in Paris? Was he asking for money? I didn't think so. That only happened outside of restaurants, not inside.

I responded in English, with something like, "Sorry, I don't understand what you are saying." As soon as he heard English words, his face became curiously expressionless and he turned and left the restaurant. He had appeared so suddenly and so close to my table that I had not noticed his baggy, grimy pants, nor his darkened, dirty, worn-out shoes. Then I understood that he *had* been asking me for money. I had never been approached by a street person inside a restaurant before.

Through the almost floor-to-ceiling windows of McDonald's, I watched him abruptly approach a businessman. With apparently no good fortune, he immediately continued across the street, and down the boulevard toward the Seine. Soon the quiet morning air he must know so well would fill with the sounds of crowds and traffic, and perhaps as the day unfolded, the man would also know success in his endeavours.

We awake to each new day with a quest or two that set our feet walking. Maybe the day begins towards a coffeemaker or a coffee shop. Maybe the day's focus centres on our job and earning a living. We set out with purpose in the morning because we have something important to go after.

As Christians, we tend to have a good grasp of the importance of seeking God in the morning. It's a principle we've known for years. But it's difficult to do and the difficulty begins as soon as we wake up. How does one quiet the mind in the loud, rushing, demanding world we live in?

Jesus knew this struggle:

Very early in the morning, while it was still dark, Jesus got up, left the house and went off to a solitary place, where he prayed. Simon and his companions went to look for him, and when they found him, they exclaimed: "Everyone is looking for you!"

—Mark 1:35-37

It can seem to us, too, that everyone is looking for us. People depend on us, and screens wait to light up so they can reveal the list of emails waiting for our response. But there is also a quiet place waiting for us somewhere, a quiet place where God will meet with us if we draw aside to seek Him. It's our choice how we start the day. Even on those most chaotic mornings, where perhaps our only quiet moment seems to be a brief look out of the window before we dash out, or a moment when sitting at a red light. Even those moments can be rich when we fully turn to God who understands us and who is the God of peace, not chaos. He can shower His peace over us. He can graciously give us the very things we need to sustain us through the quests we set for ourselves.

David met with God in the morning with purpose and an open heart:

Listen to my words, Lord, consider my lament. Hear my cry for help, my King and my God, for to you I pray. In the morning, Lord, you hear my voice; in the morning I lay my requests before you and wait expectantly.

—Psalm 5:1-3

Isaiah also writes with a great sense of purpose about the morning:

The Sovereign Lord has given me a well-instructed tongue, to know the word that sustains the weary. He wakens me morning by morning, wakens my ear to listen like one being instructed.

—Isaiah 50:4

The world in the times of David and Isaiah was no more peaceful than our world today. David woke up to sigh and cry out to God for help. Isaiah woke up to listen and learn so that he could comfort weary people. We wake up needing God's help for ourselves and to equip us to minister to the weary world we step out into. God remains the same faithful One who hears, answers and sustains us daily.

*V*isiting the places on my list consumed most of my daily routine. That list needed to remain flexible and creative, though, because some places were impossible to visit. Either they were under construction, had locked doors or simply could not be found. But there was unexpected gain. I would happen upon places that I never intended to see, such as the twelfth-century church St. Julien le Pauvre which sits near Square René Viviani. In that square, I discovered the oldest tree in Paris, planted in 1601. My plan that morning had not been to see a very old tree but simply to find the phenomenal Shakespeare and Company bookstore nearby.

Instead of returning to America right after his service with the American army during WWII, George Whitman moved to Paris and enrolled in courses at the Sorbonne. His extensive collection of books in English eventually led to the beginnings of his bookstore, Shakespeare and Company. He opened the bookstore on the Left Bank across from Notre-Dame in 1951, in what was once a three-storey apartment. It remains today as a famous cozy bookstore, where the third level serves as a comfortable, casual reading room and a writers' meeting place.

On the first floor, in the nook area underneath the stairs, I browsed the mystery section of used books, choosing a paperback by a known author. With my main quest of the day achieved, I skimmed through a stack of new books as possible gifts for my family, but I didn't buy anything else, knowing I'd be returning to Shakespeare and Company later with Hannah.

Finding the store would now be easy. I had known the store was centrally located across the river from Notre-Dame, but knowing about a location and finding it are two different things. I imagined how impressed Hannah would soon be with her mother knowing Paris so well.

I left the bookstore and neared Place St. Michel with its six busy intersections. Having been in Paris several days now and having crossed my share of busy boulevards, I knew to take care before stepping off the curb, to ensure that all the drivers, even the impetuous ones, had indeed stopped at the red light.

When I first arrived in Paris and approached another busy intersection along the Seine, I had crossed it incorrectly. Across the many angled traffic lanes, I saw the glowing green 'walking man' signal light up and had confidently stepped off the curb. The problem was that because of the way many roads met the intersection, I hadn't noticed that the medians between the lanes each had their own pedestrian light and that they were to be properly negotiated one median at a time. The glowing green sign that I had wrongly taken as my cue began to blink at me far off in the distance, but I still had a long way to go, to finish crossing the street. *They've got to be kidding! How do they expect me to cross this road in two seconds?* I hurried across, aware that the oncoming traffic of the last two lanes stared down at me, having been released from their red light. Thankfully I had enough time to scurry out of the way.

My mistake had been in looking at a signal too far ahead. Looking too far into the distance can be a problem. Focusing on the wrong thing way up ahead means that the things in between are often missed. And what is in between can be critical. It can be what actually gets you successfully to the goal ahead.

Trying to tackle too much distance all in one go is not a wise approach to travel. We travel a certain distance but then we sense that we need to stop. We need to prepare for the next part of our journey and it's critical to heed such warning signals.

Preparation along the way is a big part of successful journeying in life, too. God expertly prepares us for what is ahead. He is always teaching us and preparing us, as He did with the Israelites when He led them to the Promised Land. It would not be a quick straightforward dash across the land.

Many lessons lay ahead for the Israelites, especially about God. Who was He? In fact, who was this Moses, the man God had sent to lead them? Their journey began with the crossing of the Red Sea. *"When the Israelites saw the mighty hand of the Lord displayed against the Egyptians, the people feared the Lord and put their trust in him and in Moses his servant"* (Exodus 14:31). The crossing of the Red Sea became an important milestone for the Israelites to remember, but also for the surrounding nations who heard about it and suddenly feared this God of Israel. But the Israelites wavered in their fear of God. On their journey, they refused to be taught. *"The Lord said to Moses, 'I will rain down bread from heaven for you… In this way I will test them and see whether they will follow my instructions'"* (Exodus 16:4). Some obeyed and some didn't.

In the end, the Israelites never got to the point of being prepared enough. Their continuing disobedience caused them to spend forty years wandering in the wilderness. God waited for one generation to pass, and the next generation to grow up before sending them into the Promised Land, under the leadership of Joshua. How sobering to think that we're not going anywhere until we've learned today's lessons. There is enough to keep us occupied here and now, and only when we're ready will God move us on to cross the next street.

I'm challenged reading the words in the epistles about getting prepared:

- *"Those who cleanse themselves from the latter will be instruments for special purposes, made holy, useful to the Master and prepared to do any good work."* (2 Timothy 2:21)
- *"Preach the word; be prepared in season and out of season…"* (2 Timothy 4:2)
- *"Always be prepared to give an answer to everyone who asks you to give the reason for the hope that you have…"* (I Peter 3:15).

Paris has some crazy streets. Fast traffic constantly circles the Arc de Triomphe, darting off into any one of its twelve adjoining streets. It's an endless flow and is fascinating to watch. If I knew nothing about Paris and was told that I'd have to walk to the Arc de Triomphe, I would panic. How could I cross that insanely busy traffic circle without risking death? But I would be able to cross when I had properly prepared. I would gather information. I would discover that there is a museum situated at the top of the Arc de Triomphe and so people are able to cross safely. Instructions would be available and I would learn that I should circle to the north of l'Arc, above the Champs-Élysées. I would then proceed down the stairs, take the underground passage and cross safely to the Arc de Triomphe, because I had prepared.

*I*n Paris, I often found myself in situations where I was tempted to stray off a main road, to wander down an obscure path. I wondered sometimes if that was wise.

Christians are warned against getting sidetracked, and it would be unwise to stray from the course that God has set us on: the path of righteousness. That's the one that the psalmist prayed about: *"Teach me your way, O Lord; lead me in a straight path"* (Psalm 27:11). Isaiah taught, *"The path of the righteous is level; you, the upright One, make the way of the righteous smooth"* (Isaiah 26:7).

It's that wide, smooth, level path of right living that we should not stray from. *"Whoever strays from the path of prudence comes to rest in the company of the dead"* (Proverbs 21:16). I didn't want any part of resting in the company of the dead.

But some of the physical paths I chose to walk in Paris were the opposite of the smooth, level and straight. In fact, I found it important to deliberately step *away* from the straight, concrete road and choose other paths. Some paths off from the main boulevard struck me as curious. Of course, I had heard the old saying that 'curiosity killed the cat', but sometimes I have wondered whether, in being so careful, I wasn't killing curiosity. Had curiosity become too dangerous, too childish, or too time-consuming?

In Paris, I gave in to curiosity and stepped off of the main road several times. I always felt a sense of hesitation because in doing so I had to cross a line that I had drawn for myself or step out of a box that I had constructed.

There were always barriers in my mind to leap over. But once on my way, these moments become rich ones, among those I remembered most. In Paris I stepped into curiosity and initiated some wonderful moments.

The Pantheon doors would open at 10:00 a.m. and I joined the small line-up that began at 9:30. After a few minutes, I made the choice not to wait any longer. I stepped out of the line and ventured up a road that wound past St. Etienne du Mont. I didn't want to get too far away from the Pantheon for fear of getting lost, but when I crossed a cobblestone road, a row of buildings blocked the Pantheon's huge dome. One more road and corner, and I no longer knew in which direction the Pantheon lay. Another corner and suddenly the dome of the Pantheon rose over the roofs—something that seemed impossible! The dome should not be there—at least, not according to my sense of direction. It reminded me of being nine years old on family vacations, and being mystified at optical illusion sites such as the Oregon Vortex. How could it be? But this wasn't some strange phenomenon; it was just me getting lost in the Latin Quarter.

I strolled up the quiet road and in turning the corner, I entered a different era. Traffic had seemingly yet to travel on the cool stones. The morning shade still darkened the shops which had yet to open for the day, save one café. Under the small café's colourful canopy sat a group of seven or eight elderly gentlemen in casual coats and scarves, bantering back and forth in conversation as wisps of steam rose from small espresso cups. These old men belonged to that space and time as much as the stones and bricks themselves, an innate part of the landscape. Before walking past, I hung back for a moment to watch, not ready to impose myself even on the sidelines of this genuine picture of Paris in the morning.

An alleyway runs narrowly between rows of historic brick buildings rising up two and three storeys high. It is certainly not wide enough for a car. It wasn't important, one late afternoon, for me to find a shortcut to the sunny block leading to another busy street and more shops. But the alley itself held a peculiar fascination. Should I? Strolling rue Saint-André-des-Arts had proven to be a pleasant time, but the alley, where sunlight failed to reach, was too intriguing.

Leaving the clamour of St. André, I disappeared into this somewhat darker place of Paris history. I stepped along, avoiding the trickle of water that ran down the centre of the alley. Piles of crates were stacked outside some back doors of shops. Like a little kid, I was compelled by an open door to peer inside, to see the bustle and hear the noises from the back workings of this shop or that café.

I reached the alley's end where I could see the sidewalk and sunlight. Alerted to a sudden movement from behind, I jumped around a stack of crates, flattening myself against a dirty brick wall to allow a sudden racing motorcycle sufficient room. I didn't venture down another narrow alley in Paris. If I ever do, I'll be wiser to watch out for their surprises.

Pont Neuf, the oldest bridge in Paris, dating back to the early 1600s and the reign of Henry IV, spans the Seine, connecting the island Île de la Cité with the Left and Right Bank. Crossing Pont Neuf, I stopped to study the grand equestrian statue of Henry IV. Stopping made me realize how tired my feet were, but I didn't want to backtrack to sit at one of the turreted bench areas on the bridge.

Instead, I sought a place to rest that would be on my way. I passed the statue on the bridge side and discovered below by the water a small green oasis amid the surrounding concrete. Park benches, tall lush trees, little flowerbeds; it was a perfect place. But how did one get down there? The answer wasn't obvious and so I decided to continue, hoping to find a park bench where navigation wasn't required.

Then, noticing a few people descending from view past the statue of Henry IV, I decided not to give up so easily. I headed over and found the set of stairs. At the bottom, an ice cream vendor operated. It was even more perfect than I had thought. A narrow path between two tall concrete walls took me through to the entrance of Square du Vert-Galant by the Seine.

I found an unoccupied bench in the sun and ate my ice cream cone. Once that disappeared, my hands held onto nothing. They rested on my purse where my camera remained tucked away inside. I leaned back, stretched out my legs, and crossed my ankles. Nothing disturbed those moments, not even thoughts of Paris today, or its history. Tall leafy trees, green grass and blue sky encompassed me. I could have been sitting in my backyard. Closing my eyes I tilted my face up towards the sun, incredibly relaxed. No longer was I a tourist in Paris, but just someone who slipped away into summertime.

God created us to be curious, inquisitive and not to give in to fear. *"The Lord makes firm the steps of the one who delights in him; though he may stumble, he will not fall, for the Lord upholds him with his hand"* (Psalm 37:23-24).

he routine of each day kept me on the lookout for souvenirs to bring back for family and friends. It made sense to get some personal shopping accomplished before Hannah arrived. But I also wanted to familiarize myself with intriguing shopping spots I knew Hannah would love to see.

Souvenirs were never far away. On both sides of the river from Notre-Dame down to the Louvre, a slow-moving crowd often developed. Along the sidewalk above the Seine, rows of forest-green wooden kiosks nudged up against the concrete edge. Each individual wooden booth held its own rough charm whatever merchandise it displayed, new and shiny or old and dusty. It's a great place to purchase trinkets like keychains, pens, coasters and fridge magnets. Some kiosks held more interesting pieces like old posters, postcards and books.

Along Quai des Grands Augustines, not far from Notre-Dame, a series of souvenir stores are jammed together with their mass-produced goods bulging out onto the sidewalk. Once inside, I felt instantly transported back to North America. Being overwhelmed with stuff, I could hear my dad's voice from long ago say, "It's so crowded in here; you need to leave just to change your mind."

A small shop close to my hotel, off the beaten tourist path, became one of my favourite souvenir stores. It contained some lovely 'touristy' items that other stores didn't have. The friendly owner was helpful and generous with his time. I could move around his store without bumping into anything.

One warm evening, after accumulating a number of souvenirs, I knew I didn't have miles to travel to my hotel, but it felt like it. I passed by the stairs leading down to the Métro, having unwisely convinced myself by that point in my vacation that, despite sore feet, walking was always the better way to go.

(Early on, I had taken the Métro, stopping at Les Halles station to transfer. A gigantic underground network in its own right, Les Halles was undergoing renovations at that time. I descended to the depths, seeking— to no avail—the correct location of my connecting Métro line. In Canada, we had grown up saying that if we dug deep enough into the ground, we would end up in China. Here in Les Halles, with Paris seeming so far above me, I sensed that I could almost hear the eerie empty expanse of the vast Pacific. I abandoned the idea of transferring and left Les Halles. I won't say that the ordeal in escaping such a subterranean network had me bolting up stairs and careening around corners in desperation for air and sunshine, but it was something close to that. I had lost my interest in the Métro, and walking became my means of transportation.)

On that tiring evening, carting my bags of souvenirs to my hotel, I cheered up knowing my favourite street, rue de la Huchette, made up part of my journey. It is old, old Paris of medieval times. The street and adjoining streets span only several metres, wide enough for one car, something that rarely appeared. Should a car approach, the unconcerned crowds would casually shuffle aside.

The narrow streets are constricted even more by the protruding display tables outside shops, and the artistic sandwich boards advertising their French, Greek or Italian restaurants. Tourists are attracted to window displays of fresh produce, bakery and exquisite wines. Not only do the streets fill, the atmosphere is full of culture, and the air is full of music and enticing aromas. Everything is bursting and alive.

After dinner and shopping, I left the life of rue de la Huchette and continued along a few less vibrant streets. It had been a good day. I had toured churches and historic sites, shopping as I went. I had been out for twelve hours. My purse, stuffed with purchases, hung heavily on my shoulder. I carried bags containing other gifts, such as chocolates from a wonderful little shop.

Had anyone been travelling with me, I'm sure I would have muttered some negative comments at that point: *I'm tired; my feet hurt; I probably haven't bought enough for so and so; maybe I should have bought that instead; I should have filled up my water bottle; I should have worn those other sandals today; are we there yet?*

Travelling alone, I kept those thoughts to myself.

How easy it is to complain about everything. How easy it is to grumble and murmur. When I read about the Israelites in the desert complaining, I've thought many times that I would fit right in. *"All the Israelites grumbled against Moses and Aaron, and the whole assembly said to them, 'If only... Why is the Lord... ? Wouldn't it be better... ? We should..."* (Numbers 14:2-4).

I thought back to the Phillip Brooks quotation that had been so striking before I left home: "I pray not for a lighter load but for a stronger back." I physically straightened up and soldiered up the street to my hotel with good posture, every muscle working hard, back, arm, and leg muscles.

How easy to complain in the midst of plenty. Paul talks about the secret of being content in every situation, even in the situation of having much. He knew how to live in plenty and the secret to it:

> *I know what it is to be in need, and I know what it is to have plenty.*
> *I have learned the secret of being content in any and every situation,*
> *whether well fed or hungry, whether living in plenty or in want. I can*
> *do all this through him who gives me strength.*
> —Philippians 4:12-13

The secret is Christ.

Strength is needed no matter the situation. It is Christ who empowers us to live in our circumstances, to live and not complain. Any transition from having plenty to being in need, or being in need to having plenty is a huge challenge physically, mentally and spiritually. It's a challenge to handle our circumstances in a way that pleases God. He gives and he takes away.

"Keep your lives free from the love of money, and be content with what you have, because God has said, 'Never will I leave you; never will I forsake

you'" (Hebrews 13:5). So it's good to know contentment with God alone because He will always be there and will not change.

The Greek word translated 'content' in this verse is '*arkĕō*' meaning 'enough, be sufficient'. It is also based on the idea of raising a barrier. You are no longer accepting any more for yourself, nor are you in pursuit of more because you are content. Nothing more is needed or wanted. You have no concerns about yourself. You are content with what you have because you have God.

My sore feet took me up to my hotel room where I unloaded my purse and bags. Later, I reviewed my budget and compared my accumulation of purchases with the size of my suitcase. It was necessary to remind myself that I was only buying a few things for a few people and not Christmas shopping for the world. I had pretty well spent enough and bought enough, and needed to be content with that; and to raise the barrier against more.

Inside St. Etienne du Mont

Lost in the Past

"All that is gold does not glitter,
Not all those who wander are lost;
The old that is strong does not wither,
Deep roots are not reached by the frost."
J.R.R. Tolkien, *The Fellowship of the Ring*

"To travel is to take a journey into yourself."
Danny Kaye

"People travel to wonder at the height of the mountains,
at the huge waves of the seas,
at the long course of the rivers,
at the vast compass of the ocean,
at the circular motion of the stars,
and yet they pass by themselves without wondering."
St. Augustine

s with many historic churches, I entered the dimness of
St. Etienne du Mont prepared to be engulfed by the soar-
ing high-domed hollowness and dwarfed by the towering
grey columns. This Gothic-style church did not disappoint me. The sun
showed a cheery warmth through the stained-glass windows, especially
the ruby red facets. Two spiral staircases, ivory in colour, had been built
at each end of the rood screen that stretched high above the many rows of
chairs separating the nave from the chancel. Medieval churches commonly blocked the laity from any sense of open access to the altar. It reminded
me that it is we who barricade the way to God. God in Christ Jesus has
opened wide the way to Himself.

Built in 1492, St. Etienne sits upon the much older foundation of
an abbey built in the fifth century. Since that time, this small area in Paris has witnessed much history. Around the year 450, Attila the Hun, in
making his rampage across Europe, even approached Paris. It is said that
Geneviève, a shepherdess, encouraged the people to pray for their city.
Inexplicably, Attila altered his course, bypassing Paris altogether. St. Etienne du Mont contains the relics and the stone base that the tomb of Saint
Geneviève once rested upon. She had been made Patron Saint of Paris but
this did not prevent her tomb from being destroyed during the French
Revolution. Today, candles burn near the stone. Rows of fresh unlit tea
light candles in casings of white, red and olive green are readily available
for anyone wanting to add their own.

Several people stood around, making it difficult to get a good view of the stone and relics. A young man in black jeans and black leather jacket hindered much of my view because he had draped his body over the stone's encasing. Even after more than 1500 years, Geneviève is still remembered, adored and perhaps even worshipped.

A few steps away from St. Etienne du Mont, the Pantheon dominates the entire landscape. Cityscape postcards highlight its huge dome towering high in the hilly district. The memory of Saint Geneviève continues here where she was first buried when the building was a sixth-century basilica. After its eighteenth century re-design in a neoclassical style, it became a national pantheon where many famous French citizens are buried. Inside, statues adorn columns and paintings decorate walls to honour men and women of the past. Wall-sized paintings, such as *Kneeling in the Woods*, show the dedication of Saint Geneviève. A series of huge paintings also depict the life of Joan of Arc. Despite the pamphlet dedicating only a small space for a sketch of the crypt below, it proved sufficient to lead me to the tombs of Voltaire, Jean-Jacques Rousseau, Victor Hugo, Alexandre Dumas, Louis Braille, and Pierre and Marie Curie.

I left the Pantheon, but remained in the Latin Quarter with a few places in mind to see. The free visitor's map snapped up at the airport and the one from the hotel lobby were not as adequate as I had hoped. Even my detailed McDonald's map failed me. Posted street signs were rare and tricky to find, often being small blue signs posted on the side of a building. Many times the identity of a street would remain a mystery.

At one point, I simply needed to cross a street to get to the other side. All three maps agreed on this. However in the physical world, three streets lay situated on the other side. Any one of them could have been the correct one leading to my destination. I chose one, knowing I was about to get lost in the Latin Quarter. Oh, to be airlifted above the maze for a quick study.

After twenty minutes of frustrating meandering, I gave up. It was time to enjoy being where I was instead of being frustrated about where I wasn't. My life would still be complete if I didn't walk the street where Ernest Hemingway worked or where George Orwell lived.

Finding a café for lunch became my imperative rather than finding addresses. Since I had already gone by several cafés, I knew another one would pop up any minute. One thing about Paris, there is always another café. I continued past more restaurants, undecided. The street then curved and the area opened to where several streets with shops and cafés converged at a small park. A couple of restaurants attracted my attention and I was soon at a sunny outdoor table, eating a ham sandwich with *frites*, watching the busyness of Paris go by.

As I started to leave, I noticed a 'rue Mouffetard' sign on the side of a building across the way. Rue Mouffetard I knew to be one of Paris's oldest roads. Thoughts clicked together. Things began to make sense. I took out a map and realized I had arrived at one of the places I wanted to find: Place de la Contrescarpe. I wasn't lost after all.

Place de la Contrescarpe was often frequented by writers like Ernest Hemingway in the early 1920s. It is the first place mentioned in Hemingway's "A Moveable Feast". Not far away is the home where he and his wife lived and where they were visited by Gertrude Stein (74 Rue Cardinal Lemoine). James Joyce and George Orwell also lived nearby. A century before them this place had a great influence on Victor Hugo who lived in Paris from 1815 to 1830.

Further back in the mid-1600s, when culture and individual expression were changing dramatically during the Renaissance, a group calling themselves the Pleiades Group formed and often met at Place de la Contrescarpe. Their interest centred primarily on the renewal of French literature and poetry.

All the while I was eating my lunch, admiring everything before me, I didn't know that I had actually arrived at the place I referred to as 'the place of the writers'.

Dozens of restaurants lined the streets and I could have stopped at any one of them for lunch. How easy it would have been to have missed this place. But I didn't. I thought about those moments of wandering around, sometimes folding my maps sloppily against the 'grain' because I had deemed them all useless—no wonder they were tearing.

I was thankful to God for not having missed seeing a place that meant so much to me.

Colossians 2:6-7 says, "*Continue to live your lives in him, rooted and built up in him, strengthened in the faith as you were taught, and overflowing*

with thankfulness." I didn't know those verses by memory, but I
moment have an overflowing sense of thankfulness, because I 1
had nothing to do with arriving at the right place. No navigational skills on
my part had taken me there. Reflecting on my frustrating route, I had to
thank God and no one else. *"Your path led through the sea, your way through
the mighty waters, though your footprints were not seen"* (Psalm 77:19).

Who but God is there to thank for such things? Those small things
that fit us so perfectly and personally? Those things that happen when we
are alone, maybe even lost? Indeed they are small things but they hit us
with a high voltage of excitement. And even though they might not hit
others with nearly the same impact, we need to accept the encouragement
we received from God and say, 'thank You.'

God knows all the minutest of details of lives lived, like those of Saint
Geneviève, Joan of Arc, Voltaire, Victor Hugo, and Ernest Hemingway. He
knows all about their footsteps around the Place de la Contrescarpe. Even
though I have no renown, He also knows my footsteps here in this area.
He knows about every one of our footprints, even the ones we'll make
tomorrow. God won't let us be lost. He will lead us and He knows how to
encourage us along the way.

chapter 15
Number Unknown

*L*ittle shops and boutiques, situated along busy streets such as rue de Rivoli, and Boulevards St. Michel and St. Germain seek attention from the passersby with exquisite window displays of clothing, confectionaries (especially chocolate) and, of course, perfumes. I passed by a collection of French perfumes beautifully displayed in the window. The display provided each bottle generous space, telling the onlooker how valued each perfume must be. The windowpane and bottle glass couldn't hold back the scented memories of the unmistakable Chanel perfumes.

Being in Paris again had triggered many memories of being here twenty years before. But I hadn't thought about my first time in Paris. That was such a different time, a different life. That was Paris in the seventies and I was eighteen years old, having just graduated from high school. I had taken the opportunity to travel with my high school friend and her family to England. During those five weeks, we took a hovercraft across the English Channel and rode the train into Paris for a weekend.

A small bottle of French perfume would be a wonderful souvenir for myself, I had thought back then. With little money to spend, I decided I could manage to splurge on a tiny bottle. Chanel No.5 had been popular since its 1921 creation by Ernest Beaux. It was the fifth scent presented to and accepted by Coco Chanel, and so the famous perfume name came about.

Since I already possessed a bottle of the popular No.5 back home, I remember thinking I'd try a Chanel perfume of a different kind, a different number. Such a small decision, but I remember it clearly. Classrooms and school hallways no longer surrounded me. My life was changing, new roads were opening up—and that would include a new perfume.

Unaware that Chanel No.19 had been described as 'assertive' and 'daring' (nothing close to my personality), I purchased a small bottle. Choosing something beyond No.5 did exemplify a daring move on my part. In 1970, the perfumer of this number, Henri Robert, made this perfume from a composition dominated by the iris flower, to honour Coco Chanel's birthday not long before she died. Coco Chanel was born on August 19, and so came about the name of the perfume.

Touring around Paris, wearing touches of the perfume, welded Parisian memories with the scent of No.19 forever. All too soon, we had boarded the train in Paris headed for Calais. It was that summer in Paris that I had learned something important about myself, which I never knew during high school: I realized how much I loved history. Walking the halls of the Louvre, seeing the Mona Lisa, strolling around the Trocadéro in the heat of the summer sun, and adjusting to the dimness in Notre-Dame couldn't have been more enthralling.

I knew that once the vacation ended, I would be home searching for a job. My plan was to save money, and then travel to more fascinating places. Then I'd return home, work and start saving more money. That would be my life. I didn't have any depth to my life plans, but then, I also didn't realize that I was spiritually lost.

I believed in God, but not having been raised in a Christian home, I didn't know exactly who He was. I considered myself a good person, so I didn't have any concerns about eternity. Because a nearby Sunday School had fun songs and stories, I had attended as a child for several years. Then a friend invited me to join Pioneer Girls Club at a Baptist Church and I enjoyed that for a couple of years, especially earning badges. I knew about Jesus dying on the cross for my sins, and I had invited Him into my heart many times. I suppose I never thought it worked because I never became perfect. Eventually, I stopped asking and in my teen years drifted away from church. Being a basically good person, I thought, would have to suffice.

Thankfully, during these years, I had received at least a basic knowledge of Christ, through faithful people like my Sunday school teachers, Pioneer Girl leaders, and friends. They are the ones I see in this verse: *"Thanks be to God, who always leads us as captives in Christ's triumphal procession and uses us to spread the aroma of the knowledge of him everywhere"* (2 Corinthians 2:14). They were the ones who faithfully spread the knowledge of Christ, Sunday after Sunday, and Tuesday after Tuesday so that I grew up knowing Jesus was good and that He had died for my sins on the cross. They laid the foundation that God continued to build upon, guiding me and keeping me until I was ready to hear more about Jesus.

We never truly know when people are ready to hear about God, and when the fragrance of the knowledge of Christ will be a welcome aroma. The message of hope is to be spread everywhere, all the time. It would be like the anointing of Christ:

Then Mary took about a pint of pure nard, an expensive perfume; she poured it on Jesus' feet and wiped his feet with her hair. And the house was filled with the fragrance of the perfume.
—John 12:3

Looking back on my life, I'm motivated to stay involved in church ministries, because so many others did that for me as a child when I didn't have any knowledge of Christ. They began that foundation, and built it up. I believe that is what God expects me to be doing because people need to know about Him.

When my high school friend and I reached Calais and took the Sealink ship back to the shores of England, I tucked my treasured tiny perfume bottle in my suitcase. At our destination, in the small English town, I unpacked. I opened my suitcase, and the city of Paris burst out like an invisible explosion. The padded lining of my suitcase absorbed most of the leaked perfume but my bottle of Chanel No.19 lay empty. Although I didn't know it yet, it was not unlike the condition of my own life. It would be a little while yet, before I would be ready to absorb the true fragrance of the saving knowledge of Christ.

Ｏ	ne evening at my hotel, I lingered at the wooden table by the
	tiny elevator, browsing through the brochures, before taking a
	few up to my room. Once settled for the evening, I sat down
in the leather director's chair in the corner and glanced through the bro-
chures. One included exotic pictures of Versailles. Another boasted the
bright colours of Disneyland Paris, what used to be called Euro Disney.
Hannah and I had already decided not to venture outside of Paris since
there was so much to see and do within the city.

I stared at Mickey Mouse, going back in time once again, vividly remembering to delight in each moment of my vacation because I knew too
well that vacations can be interrupted.

In October 1979, I was single and twenty-one. I had good friends.
My secretarial job in an oil and gas company rolled smoothly along, and
I was earning enough for travelling. I had already been to England, Paris
and Hawaii. Besides work, adventures in far-off places, and discos, what
else mattered? From my perspective, my life was totally fine—until my
mom had an idea.

She wanted her three daughters to take a week off work and she
would send us down to Los Angeles. She would pay for the flights, hotel,
everything. But there was a catch. We would have to attend a Christian
seminar. She had just attended one in Calgary and the next one in the series would take place in L.A.

My sisters and I became increasingly concerned about our mom because of this religious stuff she was getting into. *What was happening to her? Was this some kind of cult?* Nevertheless, all three of us had a love for travelling. We wanted to go and with Mom's all-inclusive offer we figured could endure the seminar. We would also be faithful to our mom, and attend all the sessions. At least we could gain some understanding into what she was believing. Amazingly, we all managed to get a week off from our jobs on such short notice. So the three sisters flew down to Los Angeles each bearing a gift from Mom—new NIV Bibles. I looked forward to a week off work, viewing it as a holiday with palm trees, a swimming pool and a chance to explore Los Angeles. A little getaway before winter set in.

Two days into the conference, we found time in the late afternoon to zip over to Disneyland. At one point, I sat on a bench outside the Haunted House, feeling extremely miserable. I was lost—not physically, since I knew roughly where my sisters were. This lost feeling had to do with my life's direction, or more accurately the fact that I didn't have one. The seminar had my mind swirling with an unsettled mess of information, Bible verses, and questions. This was not the holiday that I had anticipated. I sat on the bench feeling miserable in the 'happiest place on earth'. If God was my heavenly Father, I thought then He wasn't like earthly fathers, because He didn't care if I had fun at Disneyland.

I began to see that my life had slowly been unraveling long before I came to L.A. I had been out of high school for a year and a half, and still had no significant plans for my life. There seemed nothing important to do. My life didn't stand on anything solid.

It was almost the end of the year, the end of the Seventies, and the end of disco. I wondered if maybe there was something new for me, something significant that would give me place and purpose.

I had no purpose.

I sat outside the Haunted House deeply unhappy, and I returned to Canada much the same way.

After a few weeks being depressed, I had enough, and made a decision. I prayed to God, still unsure who He was, but asking Him to guide me and especially to teach me. The depression began to lift. I called my mom and we talked about churches. Soon I would understand she had become an incredible woman of great faith.

I opened the phone book to the yellow pages. Since Pioneer Girls had been fun, I felt that I'd try the nearest Baptist church. The next Sunday, address in hand, I nervously entered the church doors. On the visitor's card, I checked off almost everything. Everything sounded so critical: Yes, I would like to become a Christian. Yes, I would like to be baptized. Yes, I would like to join the church. Yes, I would like prayer.

I didn't check off the box about wanting a visit from a pastor or an elder because I knew I would return the next week. In my heart I had committed myself to attending church. Visitors from the church came anyway, and it was an extraordinary visit because, as I was ministered to, for the first time I understood Ephesians 2:8-9:

> *For it is by grace you have been saved, through faith—and this is not from yourselves, it is the gift of God—not by works, so that no one can boast.*

I wasn't basically good, not even occasionally good in and of myself, and it was useless trying to work at it. Christ, the only One who was good, solely provided for my salvation. I needed to trust Jesus. I couldn't reach a level of goodness on my own, but once I accepted Christ's forgiveness of my sins provided through His death on the cross, then I would be seen by God as if I were perfect. What a magnificent plan that only a sacrificial God could or would provide.

It has been more than thirty-five years since that day and I'm still attending the same church.

Three decades ago, God didn't say to Himself, "Hmmm, I'd better not bother her right now—she's in Disneyland." No—God interrupted not only what I thought would be a nice little vacation, but also what I perceived to be a nice little life. *"As the heavens are higher than the earth, so are my ways higher than your ways and my thoughts than your thoughts"* (Isaiah 55:9).

We can't predict how a holiday is going to go. Some vacations take on an adventurous tone that we never expected, while others flow quietly along. And some vacations are life-changing, because we are lost and need to be found.

*W*alking around the famous cemetery la Cimetière du Père-Lachaise was like strolling through a miniature land. In this 'neighbourhood' of small-scale houses, one dead resident lies beside another. Each door without a doorknob keeps death locked inside. The Bible speaks of this:

> *For all can see that the wise die, that the foolish and the senseless also perish, leaving their wealth to others. Their tombs will remain their houses forever, their dwellings for endless generations, though they had named lands after themselves.*
> —Psalm 49:10-11

I had entered one of the world's largest cemeteries containing 70,000 tombs. For an hour I walked on narrow brick paths, following rows of well-established ornate mausoleums, vaults, concrete graves and headstones. Pockets of less defined graves marked by crosses, stones and pillars were clustered together, making it difficult to distinguish one burial site from another.

Ground level views at every turn revealed only nature's dullest of colours. Then, unexpectedly showcased in the sunlight, I would see brilliant green moss thriving on the other side of a bleak gravestone.

Rounding a mausoleum, another surprise came to me with the sudden appearance of two quiet tourists. It was startling to remember that I wasn't the only body here that moved.

After an hour of meandering along with the cemetery map, I still had not come across one dead person on my list. To make it on my list was a simple matter: the person had to have a name I had heard of before, and preferably knew something about. Obviously, despite my reading of French history to prepare for Paris, I still lacked in general historical knowledge.

The famous gravesites of Gertrude Stein, Oscar Wilde and Georges Seurat were in divisions at the farthest corner from where I stood. Graves like those of Delacroix, Haussman and Jim Morrison were closer, although with almost 109 acres to cover, nothing was close.

Some strategically planted leafy trees kept the walk cool, but to sit down, I had to step out into the hot sunlit green space to a bench that provided a hazy westward view of Paris.

There is a melancholy weariness about cemeteries, despite how fascinating they can be. Death is naturally on one's mind. And it's difficult when touring a cemetery, not to wander off mentally, getting lost in cemeteries of the past, ones you initially entered out of necessity, not out of interest. Every once in a while, you find yourself standing there again.

East of Calgary lies a cemetery vastly different from la Cimetière du Père-Lachaise. The head markers sit flat like the open prairie land with nothing to block the wind. In the section called The Garden of the Apostles, my dad was buried on a cold brisk autumn day. It was almost thirty years ago, and it seemed such a long time since then when I was twenty-six.

In a different cemetery north of Calgary, the day grew hot and dry in the July summer sun eight years ago when we gathered around for my brother's interment.

Two-and-a-half years ago, I returned to The Garden of the Apostles in January. Flowers flowing over the casket captured my focus, allowing me to forget the arctic air blowing down into my bones. A man in black standing against the winter white reached out to retrieve several peach carnations. He gave me one before my sister's casket was lowered.

Seven months later, for two days at the care home, my mom drifted away. Her breathing became even shallower. Then she breathed her last breath. A warm September breeze blew across the flat headstones in The Garden of the Apostles as we buried her.

I grew up in a large family of nine: two parents, four brothers and two sisters. And now, there are only five of us left. Even though we all have our own families now, life still holds a painful emptiness about those losses, felt at different times, in different places.

But now it was time to get out of the heat and leave all the cemeteries my mind and body had occupied. It was time to get to other places in Paris. The path I chose for my exit worked well and took me past the graves of Frédéric Chopin and Camille Pissaro.

As I left, I passed several statues. A deep patina coated their aged bronze so that they appeared as daunting figures hewn from unpolished jade. But the more I stared at them, the more they appeared depressing rather than daunting. One tall statue in her long robes towered over me in great despair, with her head lowered, her hand covering her eyes, unable to look at death, yet unable to distance herself from it.

For over a hundred years, another female statue has sat quietly nestled up against the side of another headstone. They were one and the same shade of green. She sat with legs tucked underneath and head leaning against the stone. She's looking down in concentration with her fingers upon the grass, as if to twirl a single blade, but with her thoughts far away.

Farther down, a gravestone stood smothered by the statue of a grieving woman. Half her body lay on the top of the stone with one arm desperately reaching out to a far corner. Her other arm was curved around her head so that she faced down, her grief hidden, poured out into the grave. Her robe revealed her lithe shape—arms, waist and legs that moved no longer because death had come to someone she knew.

These women can't leave the cemetery. They remain solidified, attached to the gravestones, lost in their grief, unable to move on. These statues don't feel life like I do. They have no discernment for the seasons in the cemetery. I feel the snow, the sun and the autumn breezes. I know the seasons will change because life moves forward. Grief and sadness still come to me, but when I enter the cemeteries of my life, I also leave them. There is life beyond and Christ gives me the strength to live my life.

"I have come that they may have life, and have it to the full" (John 10:10).

I am the resurrection and the life. The one who believes in me will live, even though they die; and whoever lives by believing in me will never die. Do you believe this?

—John 11:25-26

chapter 18
Ancient Stones

*T*he museum held fascinating treasures in every room and corridor. Yet nothing compared with walking through the dimly
lit hallway, down stone stairs into the cavernous ancient room
that housed the fascinating first-century Roman thermal baths. The museum on Boulevard St. Michel was physically built around these Roman
baths, as evidenced outside by a protective wire fence around an opening
of the active archeological site where people were still exploring and making discoveries among the Roman remains. The museum also included the
adjoining nineteenth century Hôtel des Abbés de Cluny.

These first-century Roman baths had probably been used for the two
centuries of Roman occupation. Well-designed rooms contained baths
specifically for the various water temperatures: cold, tepid and hot. On a
lower level, rooms served for administration, storage, laundry and sewage.

Some refer to this museum as the Cluny Museum, but it is also called
the National Museum of the Middle Ages. The Middle Ages began around
the beginning of the sixth century when the Roman Empire fell. The Empire had ruled since Julius Caesar in the first century B.C., and it came to
rule most of the land bordering the Mediterranean Sea, including Judea,
as we know from Luke 2:1: *"In those days Caesar Augustus issued a decree
that a census should be taken of the entire Roman world."*

In the first century A.D., the large northwestern portion of the Roman Empire was called Gaul, which is today's France. In Gaul, a small settlement called Lutetia developed, later becoming Paris.

Besides these Roman baths, other remnants of the Empire exist also in the Latin Quarter. I crossed rue Monge where a shaded path ran along an ancient stone wall. The trees along a path abruptly gave way to an intimidating stone entrance that led to a vast open space. An engraved plaque read: *"Arènes de Lutèce ou les joutes nautiques succedaient aux luttes de gladiateurs, les combats de fauves a la representation des comedies et des drames."* (This can be roughly translated as: "The Lutèce Arena, where mock naval battles were followed by gladiator combats, wild animal fights and the presentation of comedies and dramas.")

I walked into the Arènes de Lutèce, a Roman amphitheatre, looking up at rebuilt steep stone seats where, two thousand years before, the arena had held 10,000 spectators. Around the arena, some individuals, a few couples and a few small groups sat on the stone seats. A number of them stared at me, the new arrival in the arena. I was small and insignificant but noticed. Climbing up to find a less vulnerable position, I moved along a cold stone row to take a seat overlooking the arena's huge circular floor of white sand. Children are known to play soccer here and old men play boules (a game similar to lawn bowling) but no one was playing that day.

Eventually I descended and crossed the arena to the exit. I purposefully gave thought to the ground I was crossing. My imagination opened to thoughts of those gladiator fights and wild beasts being hunted. I felt relieved to step out of that space.

Not far from the amphitheatre lay a narrow winding cobblestone road. Rue Mouffetard is known as one of Paris's oldest roads, one that was also built during Roman times. Not all roads lead to Rome but this one originally did, leading south toward Italy.

In the second century, the Roman Empire grew with more territory added under Trajan. But eventually the Empire began to weaken. In Lutetia, Barbarians put an end to the Roman baths and destroyed the Arènes de Lutèce as early as the third century. The Roman Empire, like the rue Mouffetard, had a beginning and an end. The dominating rule of the Roman Empire fell apart in the fifth century.

In Paris lie these many remnants of an authority that once dominated maps of the entire Western world. Coloured portions on maps show its progress over the centuries. But even at its height, the empire had always been confined by lines, borders and time.

While sitting in the amphitheatre, looking across to the other curved row of seats, I had thought not only about the Romans, but also about Christ. He had willingly come to submit to Roman authority: "*And being found in the appearance as a man, he humbled himself by becoming obedient to death—even death on a cross!*" (Philippians 2:8)

The Jewish leaders didn't have the authority to put Jesus to death. They had to bring Him before the Romans. At the time of Jesus' crucifixion, Pilate was the Roman governor of Judea.

> *Pilate said. "Don't you realize I have power either to free you or to crucify you?" Jesus answered, "You would have no power over me if it were not given to you from above."*
> —John 19:10-11

The Romans had authority only because God granted it to them for a time. But Christ's authority didn't end in stones that you study in archeological digs to understand His past, or in stone replicas that you sit upon and reflect on what once was. When I think of Christ's authority and His Empire, I think of one stone in particular. It too was sat upon but it had nothing to do with the end of His reign. "*There was a violent earthquake, for an angel of the Lord came down from heaven and, going to the tomb, rolled back the stone and sat on it*" (Matthew 28:2). This was not a remnant stone of a past historical figure. The stone that sealed the tomb needed to be rolled out of the way, not so that Jesus could get out, but so that we would know that He had risen from the dead and that His authority over everything and everyone would never end.

> *The angel said to the women, 'Do not be afraid, for I know that you are looking for Jesus, who was crucified. He is not here; he has risen, just as he said'.*
> —Matthew 28:5-6

He will be great and will be called the Son of the Most High. The Lord God will give him the throne of his father David, and he will reign over Jacob's descendants forever; his kingdom will never end.

—Luke 1:32-33

Hannah at the entrance to Notre-Dame

Travelling Together

"Never go on trips with anyone you do not love."
Ernest Hemingway

"A journey is but measured in friends,
rather than miles."
Tim Cahill

"We are all travellers
in the wilderness of this world,
and the best we can find in our travels
is an honest friend."
Robert Louis Stevenson

chapter 19
Reflecting at Rue Rivoli

*W*ith a view of the Louvre from a serve-yourself-style café on rue de Rivoli, I sat outside sipping my first cup poured from a pot of Earl Grey tea and munching on a chicken salad sandwich. It was a memorable hour that allowed me to reflect upon the past six days in Paris. I considered the advantages of travelling alone, remembering one particular early evening.

Place St. Michel is situated at a busy intersection by rue Danton, Boulevard St. Michel, and Quai des Grands Augustins by the Seine River. Street performers take advantage of the busy location with its open space by the fountain. It was easy for people to gather around to watch.

Towering above the fountain is a sculptured angelic battle scene in bronze of the archangel Michael and the fallen angel Lucifer. Gabriel Davioud's 1860 sculpture of Michael vanquishing Satan is a powerful image set high upon a plateau of rocks with water cascading down to a pool below.

Michael, holding a sword in one hand, has both arms raised high in the air with his mighty wings spread out behind him. He stands over Satan who has fallen, clutching the rock below and lying at Michael's feet.

Then war broke out in heaven. Michael and his angels fought against the dragon, and the dragon and his angels fought back. But he was not strong enough, and they lost their place in heaven. The great dragon was hurled down—that ancient serpent called the devil, or

Satan, who leads the whole world astray. He was hurled to the earth, and his angels with him.

—Revelation 12:7-9

Two people walking by me did not stop to watch the street performers, or to glance up at Davioud's amazing sculpture. This young couple—maybe on their honeymoon, or maybe just boyfriend and girlfriend—had their own battle going on. The sidewalk became jammed with people, trapping me into following close behind the couple. I really did not want to hear another private argument but it seemed unavoidable. She suggested going back to the hotel because he sounded to her as if he needed more sleep. He wanted to stay out because, after all, they were in Paris. He then sarcastically suggested that they should go back to the hotel to watch CNN, as if that was more exciting than exploring Paris.

The pedestrian traffic began thinning out. With their conversation matching their steps—tense and snappy—they were soon beyond earshot. I watched them as I strolled behind. Most couples in Paris keep close together side by side. This couple allowed enough of a gap between them that they were no longer recognizable as a couple. People easily passed between them. I couldn't help but feel compelled to pray for them.

The Bible says, "*Do two walk together unless they have agreed to do so?*" (Amos 3:3) The advantage to travelling alone was that I only had to agree with myself about where to walk, where to eat, and when to go back to my hotel. I poured my second cup of Earl Grey and remembered another day and another couple.

Somewhere along rue de la Roquette, near the Bastille, I had passed by a middle-aged couple. He stood, map held up in both hands, his eyes alternating quick glances from the map to the street intersection. The determination carved into every line of his face didn't allow for even a hint of a smile. She stood beside him, relaxed but involved. Calmly, she observed the intersection and then her attention went back to him.

I smiled, knowing so well, that feeling of standing perplexed on a street in Paris with an open map. Some tourists don't like to look like tourists, but these two didn't care. They may have been frustrated, but not with each other. They were lost together. And although they had come to a complete stop, I believed they would soon agree on a direction and start walking.

To travel with someone allows the experience to be shared, and to have those memories to share later on. There is someone to encourage the other when things don't go well. There is someone to laugh with. There is someone to talk to.

One thing is for sure: travelling together can't be done successfully without love:

> *Love is patient, love is kind. It does not envy, it does not boast, it is not proud. It does not dishonor others, it is not self-seeking, it is not easily angered, it keeps no record of wrongs. Love does not delight in evil but rejoices with the truth. It always protects, always trusts, always hopes, always perseveres. Love never fails.*
> —I Corinthians 13:4-8

I knew I had been blessed with a wonderful opportunity to spend time in Paris, seeing what I wanted to see at my own pace. I had seen almost everything I wanted to see and had enjoyed the past week immensely. But travelling alone can be lonely. I missed my family. Often when I saw something, I thought about how much fun they would have had being here. Over the years, our family has covered thousands of miles on road trips in North America. I've always been thankful that we've been able to travel well together as a family, not flawlessly but well, and well enough to want to plan other trips together in the future.

I ate the last of my sandwich, and poured the remaining tea. I glanced at my watch and felt excitement about seeing my daughter. Ahead lay three whirlwind days at major tourist sites that, up until now, I had only stopped to look at from the outside, always on my way to somewhere else. These sites were on the top of Hannah's list and we would see them together.

I looked out at the Louvre, amazed at its immensity. I knew which entrances to the Louvre were best to line up at, depending on the time of day. Notre-Dame's best approach would be to enter the church first thing in the morning, then head to the north side to join the lineup for the tower tours. Afterwards, by taking a short walk west from Notre-Dame, past some trees, across a street, then down a block, we would arrive at the entrance of the Conciergerie and Saint-Chapelle. Then there was always the Eiffel Tower, off in the distance, taunting me with its unknown elevator situation.

On Hannah's list (but not a high priority) was the Musée d'Orsay, where many Impressionist paintings were on display. Since it ranked high on my list, I had spent two hours there one morning and if I spent two more hours there with Hannah, it would not be a hardship. (The beauty of a museum pass allows one not only to use the express line, but also to enter a museum as many times as one wants.)

We had planned our days together and I had done some tweaking of those plans. I left the café to have ample time to figure out the Métro to Gare du Nord. I promised Hannah that I would meet her and the time had come for me to leave Paris and take the train out to the airport.

I negotiated Gare du Nord and took the train out to the airport where I found my way to the correct meeting gate in good time. Arriving passengers trickled around the corner of the corridor with inexplicably long gaps of time in between. Nothing blocked our view but the woman beside me strained her head forward each time to see the next arriving passenger. She was probably a mom like me. Then I saw Hannah: long blonde hair, blue jeans, yellow t-shirt, backpack and beautiful smile! How wonderful to wrap my arms around her in a big hug.

Parents want their children to have a better life than the one they have had. This also applies to airport experiences. I wanted Hannah's airport experience to be smooth, although it was bound to be since she was fluent in French. There was no need to stop at a visitor's desk or ticket office, or to stare blankly into a ticket-dispensing machine. I had taken care of all of those things, so I placed in Hannah's hands her train ticket to Paris, Métro tickets, a two-day museum pass, and a map of the city of Paris. We proceeded flawlessly to platform number eleven and sat on the train heading for Paris. It was a snap. Unlike my arrival in France, my daughter didn't need to hear a voice behind her. There at the airport, she had her helicopter mother hovering over her.

It's not that I didn't want my daughter to experience a sense of God's guidance. I simply wanted to have everything ready as a matter of expediency because Hannah and I had plans. And the more daylight for sightseeing, the better.

My desire is to be a good mom who will give good counsel, and to teach my children—even now that they are young adults. I want to be helpful but I know it's important not to interfere with God's plans. My children need to hear other voices besides mine.

Children need to have their own personal stories to tell. They need space to make their own errors of standing on wrong platforms, maybe sweating a bit, and then realizing that God will get them to their destination. When they are in difficult situations, they need to have personal memories to look back on, times to recall when God came through and helped them.

I'm in my fifties and still going through wrong doors and standing on wrong platforms, and God faithfully continues to get me to where I need to go in life. My children need to know how to depend on God now so that they won't fear to step out when they reach their fifties. They will have built up a reservoir of their own experiences to be encouraged by. I will fail to be with them to encourage and help, but their heavenly Father will never fail to be present with them.

On the train into Paris, Hannah shared about her trip from England. She had had to take two trains to get to the Bristol airport. She left one train to quickly jump onto the next and described it as taking a leap of faith, trusting God that it was the right train.

The train ride into Paris isn't all that picturesque but I smiled as I looked out of the window, thinking about Hannah's experience, so thankful for God and what He was teaching her. She had collected a memorial, like those stones the Israelites used to mark their entry into the Promised Land. After crossing the Jordan, the Israelites chose twelve stones, one to represent each tribe, to set up as a sign for the future to remember how God had led them. *"These stones are to be a memorial to the people of Israel forever"* (Joshua 4:7). 'Memorial' comes from the Hebrew word *'zikrôwn'*, meaning record. This is based on the idea of being marked, being able to be recognized. A pile of large stones would be easily recognized.

The memories of our experiences with God should also be easily recognizable. They need to be recorded in our journals and recounted in our witnessing so that they remain standing and visible rather than being like scattered stones covered by the water. We gather them up, an ongoing ord, so that we can go to that place and recall them, be encouraged, and share what things the Lord has done.

What can make your day any better than to hear your child talk about trusting God and taking 'leaps of faith'? *"I have no greater joy than to hear that my children are walking in the truth"* (3 John 4).

Parents who *hear about* their children were not there to see it for themselves. The joy comes from hearing, and hearing implies distance. It is news that is being given secondhand, because the parents have let go. The joy is in hearing, not in hovering.

God is the one who encircles our children; He has them in His hands.

chapter 21
Sacré-Coeur

*T*he forty-five-minute train ride gave time for Hannah and me to catch up on each other's lives. We then disembarked at the Gare du Nord. With the welcomed lingering daylight, we kept to our plan of taking the Métro to Sacré-Coeur in the Montmartre district. It is far from our hotel and most other tourist sites, and it would probably be the only time we would be able see this Basilica. But at Gare du Nord, we hit a snag: the Métro that would take us close to Sacré-Coeur was not operating. We had to improvise a Plan B quickly. Another Métro brought us close enough but it meant hiking up through Montmartre, so we began our ascent. As long as we switch-backed our way uphill, and my heart kept pumping to the extreme, we felt we must be heading in the right direction.

Trees branched over long concrete stairways and steep sidewalks. Not many people met us on this path up to Sacré-Coeur. I realized why when we reached the last step of the last stairway and saw the back of the Basilica. We had not followed a main route that would have brought us to the grand front entrance of the layers of steps and the large foliage-engraved bronze doors.

However, arriving at the back of the Basilica had its advantages. Dwarfed by the impressive domed Roman-Byzantine-style Church, we slowed our pace, entering the important cooling-down portion of our cardio workout. We made our way along the west side of the basilica in search of the front entrance, all the while admiring the building's travertine stone. Travertine is an extremely hard stone that appears white because of the calcite content it exudes when it rains. That's why, from anywhere in Paris, this church stands out like an ancient whitish-blue castle set upon a hill.

The Sacred Heart Basilica (Sacré-Coeur) is not centuries old, but was built between 1875 and 1914. The ground, as is almost always the case, holds so much more history. Here, in the third century, the first Bishop of Paris, Saint Denis, arrived to preach to the Gauls, and was decapitated for his faith. A chapel built here in the fifth century in honour of St. Denis eventually had to be rebuilt in the ninth century.

This became a place of pilgrimage to honour St. Denis and many other Christian martyrs. Later on, because of war between Germany and France in 1870, part of France became occupied by Germany. In 1872, a vow was made to build a church in penance for all the misfortunes that had befallen France, and so the plans for Sacré-Coeur began. Today, it still is a place of pilgrimage.

We reached the front of Sacré-Coeur. With mixed emotions, I surveyed the many tourists who had arrived so effortlessly by tour bus. We found our place in the long line-up at the stairs. There, we could easily view the two large bronze equestrian statues of national saints outside the basilica's doors, those of Joan of Arc and King Louis IX. Only small groups could enter at a time, and when we finally neared the front doors, our group began its turn shuffling through. We concentrated on everything, aware that photography was not permitted. At a slow pace, we viewed the magnificent domed building, pillars, windows, gold mosaics, and especially the image of Christ up high, arms open wide.

Back outside, small clusters of people were sprinkled upon the wide expanse of steps that provided a fantastic view of the cityscape of Paris spread out below. We joined the crowd and spent some moments in the pleasantness of the warm early evening, sitting on the steps of the Basilica.

A unique feature of Sacré-Coeur is that for over 130 years, night and day, there have been prayers offered, along with an ongoing Eucharist, and a priest is always on site. The emphasis is on prayer for the revealing of the love of God to all people, and prayers for forgiveness.

Not able to hop on a tour bus like the rest of the travellers, Hannah and I began our descent into Montmartre, following a path we discovered near the front of the church. It would have been pointless to try to retrace the convoluted route we had hiked up. We aimed at finding the same Métro station, and if not, at least the same main street.

Because of the need to hike up to the Basilica, we had spent more daylight than we had anticipated. An awareness of impending darkness became painfully obvious. As good as an idea of seeing Sacré-Coeur was, I wondered whether we should have tried to somehow fit it in on a different day, in daylight. It didn't prove helpful to think about that while descending the ever-darkening streets of Montmartre. Hopefully we would run into the Métro line soon.

In the span of three blocks, only two pedestrians passed us. No cars, no bicycles. Across the road, the vacant sidewalk joined with dull stone walls overhung with eerie tree branches. Sometimes the stone walls gave way to gates, halfway opened to gloomily lit dwellings where no movement could be seen inside. The darkness grew uncomfortable and the deserted streets unnerving. We had entered the opening pages of a thriller novel, set in hilly Montmartre which means 'Mount of Martyrs'. Around the corner down the third block, our surroundings were no cheerier.

This was not how I wanted to begin the vacation with my daughter, imagining us getting mugged or murdered. I felt like such an irresponsible parent. How much better things would have been had we had one extra hour.

There were moments on our descent, during pauses in our chatting, that I prayed several silent 'keep us safe' prayers. The psalmist prayed such prayers: *"Let all who take refuge in you be glad...Spread your protection over them, that those who love your name may rejoice in you"* (Psalm 5:11). To ask for God's protection to be spread over us seemed a reasonable request.

Walking in such bleakness, I imagined hilly Montmartre in a different setting: in the bright daylight, over a century ago, when well-known artists lived and worked here, honing their skills. Montmartre was home to the likes of Pierre-August Renoir, Toulouse-Lautrec, Henri Matisse and Vincent Van Gogh, with their canvases full of colours.

Van Gogh lived in Paris in 1886 to 1888, and for a time, concentrated solely on discovering colour. He wrote, "I painted almost nothing but flowers to accustom myself to a colour other than grey, that's to say pink, soft or bright green, light blue, violet, yellow, orange, fine red." Today, a

Kim Louise Clarke

vase of bright sunflowers has become synonymous with Vincent although his painting of the sunflowers that began in Paris didn't blossom into bright bunches on canvases until he left Paris to live in Arles, France.

Imagining Montmartre in bright daylight and filled with colourful canvases didn't help the present situation which called for zig-zagging down dark roads. What made a difference for me was knowing that God walked with us. David wrote about Him saying, *"You, Lord, are my lamp; the Lord turns my darkness into light"* (II Samuel 22:29).

We never know what is around the corner, but sometimes we get a sense that things are about to change. In Montmartre, the indication of approaching change came from hearing new sounds as we approached a corner. We could hear the sounds of the chattering of people and of music. Closer now, we noticed a table's edge protruding out from the side of a building. Once we turned the corner, the sight of a lively restaurant stunned us. It completely outgrew the sidewalk, spilled out onto the street, and stretched down the block. We wondered where all these people had come from. How had all this life suddenly come into being?

A few more quiet streets and a little bit more gloominess lay beyond this bright spot in our journey, but we turned more corners, and found even more lively cafés. Then the Métro line came into sight.

The warm evening air lingered. Once at our hotel, we rested from our exploits, then crossed a few streets to relax at an outdoor café along the Boulevard St. Michel. Despite the familiar American light rock tunes that drifted out of the café's kitchen, and our choice to snack on pizza, there was no doubt that I was with my daughter in Paris.

Back at the hotel later that night, I browsed through the pamphlet from the Basilica which read: "When a visitor sees the dome of the Basilica, he says to himself: 'Up there, the Lord is present. Up there, somebody is praying for me.'"

*A*fter fresh croissants and coffee at my favourite *boulangerie* the next morning we strolled into the Tuileries Garden. With museum passes in hand, I took Hannah on a quick detour through the Musée d'Orangerie, primarily to immerse Hannah in the room so fully dedicated to Monet's water lilies. This was a brief diversion since our goals that first day were to visit the Eiffel Tower and the Louvre Museum.

We ventured far enough past the Place de la Concorde to cross a special bridge, Pont Alexandre III, named after the Russian Tsar Alexander III who signed the Franco-Russian Alliance of 1892. Crossing the bridge was like entering a celebration where gilded statues and seventeen-metre-high pillars stood at both ends, and in between were adorned lampposts, sculpted cherubs and nymphs. It had been built for the World's Exposition in 1900. A tourist might not even look particularly touristy here, incessantly snapping photos, since this bridge is often seen in films and fashion shoots.

After crossing Pont Alexandre, Hannah and I continued along a broad sidewalk on our way to the Eiffel Tower. A woman appeared in front of us, seemingly from nowhere. She stooped down to pick up something from the sidewalk. Her long crinkled skirt and billowing sleeves flowed gracefully with her. She looked to be in her late forties. My eyes followed her and my understanding scrambled to catch up. Then I recognized it— although I'd never seen it before, I knew about this performance.

With an almost guilty fascination, I thought, "Oh, It's the scam! I get to see the ring scam!" I marvelled at how smoothly she picked up the ring after she had cleverly rolled it onto the sidewalk to begin with. Continuing in fluid motion, she gracefully straightened her back to stand in front of us, bringing the flattened palm of her hand before our eyes. With nefarious intent, she displayed a gold ring. How many times had she done that before? What was the life story that had brought her to such depraved perfection?

We decided right away not to get involved, and we gestured with a wave of our hands. No, we're not interested. And we carried on.

Had we stopped, the woman would hope for a typical scenario to unfold. She would exclaim that the ring must belong to us. We would politely reply, "Sorry. No, it doesn't."

To not lose her audience, she would need to keep talking, reasoning with us that someone else must have lost the ring, that it looked very valuable. She would insist that we might as well take the ring. She would hope that we would.

Then, supposing we did take the ring, she would proceed to ask us if we had a few Euros we could spare. By then, we would be feeling some measure of empathy towards her. After all, this unselfish poor woman hadn't even considered keeping the valuable ring for herself. Surely we could give her something.

The woman hoped for a happy ending. She envisioned herself disappearing with a few Euros tucked away, and us strolling away in the wonderment of potential wealth, carrying a worthless brass ring.

We were meant to be deceived by the lure of something that had the look of value. But it wasn't gold, not even fool's gold. What she had presented us with was surely an alloy—copper and zinc combined to become brass—a metal that looked like gold at a distance.

The woman couldn't have known that we were familiar with her story. I had been told about it by someone who had fallen for it, and I read several online accounts of sad ring-scam tales before leaving home. Knowing about the setup immediately alerted us to spot the falsehood. There was no need to study the ring, on the slight chance that it could be valuable. We were prepared and easily detected a scam.

But the thing about being tricked is that we never know when it will happen.

Hannah and I found that at the well-frequented tourist sites, people were adequately informed about the possibility of being pick-pocketed. Elusive thieves received a lot of press. Plenty of signage could be seen at entryways and information desks. Once, while standing in line, we watched a cartoon video high up on mounted flat screens, demonstrating clever methods of stealing your attention, your wallet, your purse.

A familiar pattern develops standing in line, chatting with those around you. You can even begin to feel part of a little group who may be targeted but who are also somewhat prepared by having been forewarned. Then on past the entry, your 'group' disbands amid the crowd heading off to different floors and exhibits. Deep inside the museum, you find yourselves immersed in artifacts, dioramas and paintings, having left all the warning signs behind. In fact, you forget all about the warnings with all the fascinating distractions, and you grow lax. You behave as if you believe that the thieves only do their work near the warning signs, and that beyond the signs you can let your guard down.

But we know that thieves don't put such restrictions on their territory. Neither should we put away our caution.

Those who have immersed themselves in spiritual trickery and falsehood have wide territories too. But God never leaves us defenseless. The Holy Spirit gives us spiritual discernment, and in Scripture we read the warning signs:

> *I urge you, brothers, to watch out for those who cause divisions and put obstacles in your way that are contrary to the teaching you have learned... By smooth talk and flattery they deceive the minds of naïve people.*
>
> —Romans 16:17-18

We watch out for such trickery by sticking together, which means keeping in fellowship with other Christians:

*If either of them falls down, one can help the other up. But pity any-
one who falls and has no one to help them up! Though one may be
overpowered, two can defend themselves. A cord of three strands is
not quickly broken.*

—Ecclesiastes 4:10, 12

We are urged to *"not give up meeting together, as some are in the habit of
doing, but encouraging one another"* (Hebrews 10:25).

Travelling with Hannah was such a welcome change: the fellowship,
the laughter, the fun, the sharing of the experience, as well as watching out
for one another. The time on my own had been amazing, but there was a
wonderfully mysterious strength I received when Hannah arrived. It is like
the church where we need to stay together and we don't have to go it alone.

*"And this is my prayer: that your love may abound more and more in
knowledge and depth of insight, so that you may be able to discern what is
best…"* (Philippians 1:9-10).

chapter 23
Yellow Cup Memories

*S*tanding at the base of one of the four massive iron legs of the Eiffel Tower is an amazing experience, and Hannah was thrilled to finally be at this historic landmark (although I don't think it compared to my delight at realizing that the elevators were functional).

I tilted my head way back to view the exposed staircase on one of the monstrous legs—a scene plucked out of someone's nightmare. People were actually ascending and descending on them, despite the working elevators. I could barely watch their movements.

Parisians take great pride in this world-famous tower, but apparently it was not well accepted when first built for the 1889 World's Fair, marking the hundredth anniversary of the French Revolution. Today, it is almost impossible to think of Paris without the Eiffel Tower.

Time in the line-up gave us time to chat about many things, including, oddly enough, Tupperware. I love Tupperware, and standing under the Eiffel Tower with Hannah brought back memories of a particular piece that I no longer have. It was a simple yellow cup with a snap-on lid with a small raised spout for a little child to sip from. I lost one in Paris in 1992. It was Hannah's.

It happened at the base of the Eiffel Tower, during our hectic passage through the entry gates, showing tickets, pushing the baby stroller through a turnstile, and moving forward with the excited crowd toward the elevator. In the chaos, I forgot to reach back to retrieve the yellow cup I had set down near the turnstile. At eight months old, Hannah was still being nursed, but also took juice and water from a cup, making things easy during our travel across Europe. The elevator doors opened for us to board. As if knowing it was taking her away from her cup, Hannah cried the entire ride up the packed elevator.

Upon exiting, I didn't look out at the lovely views of Paris. Carrying Hannah, I quickly found a place to sit among the overpowering structural iron and the chattering tourists. With the wind whipping my hair about and with clammy hands from the sudden heights, I nursed Hannah and calmed her down. Then together we looked out over the city of Paris.

Now, twenty years later, Hannah and I once again lined up at the Eiffel Tower. Thinking back to that day so long ago, we chatted about it. I described the entire scenario as if Hannah had never heard the story before. Even before Hannah left Canada, she had said that the one souvenir she had to buy in Paris would be a souvenir cup of some kind, and it had to be yellow.

Before riding to the very top, we spent time at the second level, 115 metres above ground, viewing the sights through all 360 degrees: the Arc de Triomphe, the Seine, Sacré-Coeur, Hôtel des Invalides, the Trocadéro, Notre-Dame. I also searched for the place where I had sat twenty years before to nurse my daughter. I'm not so sure that I found the right spot, but I recognized the weather. It was exactly the same as that day, sunny, pleasant and breezy.

Paris seemed overly familiar, as if I had seen these views recently, rather than two decades before. As I've said, I'm not fond of heights but there was something peaceful about being high above it all. Such distance prevents you from getting involved in the details of things. In the small space on the second level, if you are not caught up in the view, your thoughts tend to drift beyond the horizon.

How odd to be back here. Paris. So much is the same but so much has changed. When I travel now, I carry so many memories. I don't intentionally pack them as necessary to bring along, any more than I unpack them when I arrive at my destination. Memories just appear. Memories of other trips, of younger years, of people who have passed on, of children grown up. So many important, rich memories.

I returned to the stunning city views, but still didn't concentrate on Paris. What touched me instead was God's goodness in the short span of my own life's history. There were countless blessings when I think back on my years of travel. I came here to see Paris with my daughter, which I was doing, but I also saw much more. I saw a panoramic view of God in my life; His greatness and His love being so much more impressive than any city in the world could ever be. God had indeed blessed me with a wonderful family.

At the top of the Eiffel Tower with Hannah again, I knew how rich God's blessings could be. Overlooking Paris, I had a moment where I simply followed God's advice to: *"Be still, and know that I am God"* (Psalm 46:10).

Walking the hallways of the Louvre

Art and Photography

"I dream my painting and I paint my dream."
Vincent van Gogh

*"Painting is poetry that is seen rather than felt,
and poetry is painting that is felt rather than seen."*
Leonardo da Vinci

"A photograph is usually looked at—seldom looked into."
Ansel Adams

*T*he Louvre began as a fortress built in the Middle Ages during the reign of Phillipe Auguste. Over the centuries, the city of Paris grew so large that the fortress with its moat and rounded bastions proved no longer adequate. It became the residence for Francois I, and later the palace for King Louis XIV until he moved his palace out to Versailles. It wasn't until 1793 that the Louvre became a museum, first known as the Museum Central des Arts.

Hannah and I only had to line up outside the glass pyramid entrance for forty-five minutes. This iconic pyramid sits in the centre of Cour Napoleon, the 1989 entrance designed by Chinese-American architect I.M. Pei. There is simply too much to observe in every direction for the wait to become boring.

Even if the Louvre stood empty, it would be a masterpiece for photographers. It comprises four levels on three wings (the Richelieu, Sully and Denon) with each wing easily deserving a day—but if you're like us with only a morning to spare, then you pick up a museum map and do your best.

Once inside the Louvre, we headed immediately for Da Vinci's *Mona Lisa*. On our way, we climbed the great marble stairway that leads up to the *Winged Victory of Samothrace*. Eventually, we knew we would see the *Venus de Milo,* and then we would have hit our top three picks. It was as if we would then be free to slow our pace and explore as much as we could of everything else displayed in the endless hallways.

Many of the paintings were massive. Battle scenes rose larger than life. *Napoleon on the Battlefield at Eylau in 1807*, painted by Baron Antoine-Jean Gros, is five metres high and almost eight metres wide. *The Battle of San Romano,* painted by Paolo Uccello, portrays the victory of the Florentines over the Sienese in Italy in 1432. It's smaller but still huge to me at two metres high and three metres wide. Wall-sized paintings portray the wounded, the dying and the dead. They are so intense and so massive, one feels swept up into the battle.

As the centuries advanced so too did the sophistication of armour and weaponry along the hallways. Styles and colours of armour varied among French, Italian and Spanish armies. But the one thing they did have in common was that none were fail-proof.

Perhaps some of the painted soldiers might live. Others look as if their wounds were far too deep. Somehow in the chaos of the fighting, an arrow, a spear, a sword, a bullet had passed beside or through the armour, entering their flesh. Their armour had failed them. All they could do in their pain was to turn their eyes helplessly toward the other side of the canvas where a more fortunate comrade stood strong, boastful and triumphant over the body of a fallen enemy.

I always thought it clever what a king of Israel once said, *"One who puts on his armor should not boast like one who takes it off"* (I Kings 20:11). Then I remembered those words were spoken by King Ahab who married Jezebel, and I knew his cleverness only went so far (I Kings 21).

The strongest of soldiers wearing the best of armour have no guarantee of surviving a battle. They cannot control the random arrow that flies, and God ensured that such an arrow would kill King Ahab:

> *The king of Israel said to Jehoshaphat, "I will enter the battle in disguise, but you wear your royal robes." So the king of Israel disguised himself and went into battle...But someone drew his bow at random and hit the king of Israel between the sections of his armor... The blood from his wound ran onto the floor of the chariot, and that evening he died.*
>
> —I Kings 22:30, 34, 35

Physical armour can only do so much. How boastful should one be about armour that carries such a poor guarantee? There is another armour, a spiritual armour that is worth boasting about. *"Therefore, as it is written: 'Let him who boasts, boast in the Lord'"* (I Corinthians 1:31). This is the armour that we should always wear and never take off.

David knew the importance of this armour when he fought Goliath. Saul's armour was a bulky deterrent that David tried on but then took off. God had already prepared David. Once David realized this, by faith, he stepped out to meet Goliath in the armour he was already wearing. His armour was the same as that which Paul talks about in Ephesians 6:10-17: *"Finally, be strong in the Lord and in his mighty power. Put on the full armor of God"* (Ephesians 6:10-11). David stepped out in faith, not wanting glory for himself but for God alone. David said: *"All those gathered here will know that it is not by sword or spear that the Lord saves; for the battle is the Lord's…"* (I Samuel 17:47). He put his confidence in God and boasted in Him.

God's armour allows me to move freely. It suits me. It's not cumbersome. It fits well so that I can maneuver about, doing what I'm meant to do. Like David, our movements in doing God's will can be natural and unhindered.

This is what the Lord says:

"Let not the wise boast of their wisdom or the strong boast of their strength or the rich boast of their riches, but let the one who boasts boast about this: that they have the understanding to know me, that I am the Lord, who exercises kindness, justice and righteousness on earth, for in these I delight," declares the Lord.

—Jeremiah 9:23-24

O n the first floor of the Denon Wing of the Louvre hangs a massive work of art painted in 1563 by Paolo Caliari, better known as Veronese. This great canvas is almost seven metres high and ten metres wide and is entitled *The Wedding of Cana*. Originally, this painting covered a wall in the Benedictine monastery on the Venetian island of San Giorgio Maggiore.

The painting is based on the biblical account of Christ's first miracle recorded in the gospel of John. Jesus, His mother Mary, and Jesus' disciples were invited to a wedding. When the wine was gone, upon His mother's urgings, Jesus instructed the servants to fill six stone water jars with water and to take some to the banquet master. The master after tasting the wine, said to the bridegroom, *"Everyone brings out the choice wine first ... but you have saved the best till now"* (John 2:10).

In many ways, this is a picture of Christ. Christ *is* the very best. He is the Sinless Saviour of the World, who had come into the world, and whose blood would soon be shed. Witnessing this miracle gave the disciples an understanding of Jesus. *"What Jesus did here in Cana of Galilee was the first of the signs through which he revealed his glory; and his disciples believed in him"* (John 2:11).

Veronese portrays this scene not only with biblical figures and Christ sitting at the centre table, but also with figures from the artist's generation. It is an ancient wedding celebration, brought into sixteenth-century Venetian times.

Kim Louise Clarke

Veronese used vibrant expensive pigments from the Orient. Looking across the canvas, I see that there are no wedding guests in bland colours. Guests are clothed with billowing sleeves of rich olive and outer garments of cobalt blue; waves of fabric fold in glimmering ivory, garnet, auburn, coral, and Tuscan orange.

The largest work in the Louvre, such a gigantic painting could only be taken in its entirety on my camera when I stood far toward the back wall. When I viewed them later, my photos took me by surprise. Instead of just the two generations of ancient Israel portrayed in Renaissance Italy, I also saw a third generation: in my photos, I had captured a band of twenty-first century people in the foreground. This third generation, despite the oddity of their ball caps, sunglasses, smartphones and museum pamphlets, blended in well. Their bright t-shirts matched the intense colours of the biblical and sixteenth-century characters. They even covered up the bottom of the frame so as to appear to be coming and going within the wedding festivities.

Incongruously, many of my twenty-first century people appeared uninterested in the wedding feast. Few probably noticed the place settings on the long tables carefully arranged for each guest. Many seemed oblivious to the musicians so close to them. Were they aware that a miracle had taken place? Did they even notice Christ in the centre?

What importance did the entire *Wedding of Cana* scene hold for them? It had been important for the Benedictine Monastery to commission Veronese with such a great work, and important for Veronese to paint it as he did with his sixteenth-century influence. It also held value for Napoleon whose troops managed to confiscate the massive painting from the monastery on the island in 1797. After shipping it to France, and bringing it across country, he had it hung in the Louvre not long after it first opened as a museum.

Regardless which generation observes the painting, whether Veronese's, Napoleon's, or ours, the vital message remains unchanged: Christ, the Saviour, invites us to come to Him. Jesus compared His kingdom to that of a wedding, inviting all of us to come.

Jesus spoke to them again in parables, saying, "The kingdom of heaven is like a king who prepared a wedding banquet for his son ... Then he said to his servants, 'The wedding banquet is ready, but those I invited did not deserve to come. So go to the street corners and invite to the banquet anyone you find.' So the servants went out into the streets and gathered all the people they could find, the bad as well as the good, and the wedding hall was filled with guests."

—Matthew 22:2; 8-10

The parable refers to inviting people from all backgrounds and nationalities into the kingdom of God. It also emphasizes that an invitation needs to be accepted. But the strong pull of the world challenges our acceptance of these invitations.

I saw this demonstrated as a live object lesson in the Louvre. I watched my fellow tourists, including me, enter the Louvre with excitement. But once we had entered the museum, our bodily composition seemed to change into iron filings drawn by some invisible magnetic force. All volition had vanished up into the air of the glassy pyramids. The force drew us robotically down hallways and upstairs right into the room of Veronese's masterpiece. All conventions of personal space had evaporated, and the visitors crowded together, not to view the masterpiece of *The Wedding of Cana*, but to turn their backs on it. With an inner determination, the visitors arched and stood on tippy-toes to catch glimpses of the much smaller painting on the wall opposite *The Wedding of Cana*—the magnetic *Mona Lisa*.

It is what tourists do in Paris. They visit the Louvre. Leonardo da Vinci's *Mona Lisa* is the one painting they are supposed to see in the Louvre. It's believed to be a portrait of Lisa Gherardini, wife of Francesco del Giocondo, painted in Florence during the years 1503-1506. The *Mona Lisa* is a small, twenty-one-inch by thirty-inch canvas, behind bullet-proof glass, with guards never far away. It is indeed a lovely painting.

After catching their struggling and awkward photographs, many leave the room completely unaware of the huge wedding going on behind them. Unaware of the miracle performed. Unaware of the miracle they could experience in their lives if they'd only accept the wedding invitation extended to them.

chapter 26
Great Buildings

I had already accumulated many photos before Hannah's arrival. On my first few days in Paris, upon seeing a grand historic building, I'd hurriedly take out my camera. It seemed embedded deep in my subconscious that if I didn't get photos of these buildings, immediately, despite standing for centuries, they would quickly sprout legs and run away. Eventually, a calm reality took over.

By our second day together, Hannah and I had covered lots of ground, getting to places that we didn't think we would have time for. We were amassing a great collection of photos. These photos would be put on computer desktops and cellphone wallpapers; and printed for the tops of real desks and framed for real walls.

At cafés, over delicious desserts like *mousse chocolat noir* and tasty sips of *boisson chocolatée*, we would look over our digital collection. Dining in restaurants, between bites of exquisite *confit de canard* (duck) or *escalope veau* (veal), we would review our next course of action, preparing for more photos by adjusting the camera for night settings or putting in a fresh battery.

Taking photographs, especially in popular tourist places, was not always easy to do. I found that crowd scenes provided a certain dynamic ambiance, telling us that on a global scale, we were in the place to be. But other than photographing the occasional well-placed crowd scene, people usually got in the way.

It was like that at the magnificent Sainte-Chapelle, which attracted volumes of tourists gazing up at the over six thousand square feet of stained glass windows, portraying over a thousand biblical figures. A panoramic picture of the red and gold patterned pillars running underneath the famous windows proved impossible without including tourists, looking pillar-like themselves, planted with heads tilted upward toward the stained glass.

Glancing through hundreds of photos on my camera back at our hotel one night, I had hoped that some photos could be fixed, using the wonderful computer process of cropping. This included the photo of the man emerging from the left inside the depths of Notre-Dame as well as the person in the fluorescent orange shirt lighting up the foreground of Sacré-Coeur. To crop sidewalks and tree branches is easy. But when cutting out people, I feel tiny tinges of meanness. It's telling them that they are not important enough to warrant remaining in my photo, that I need them to disappear.

We crop because people are in the way or are taking up too much space around the focal point. We are not saying that the historical building is more important than the unknown tourist. Of course we know that people are more important than things. The challenge is to live like we believe it.

I loved all the many historic buildings and monuments in Paris that have endured through layers of time. It's that kind of historical site that I wanted to have printed and framed. Although I wasn't there for any of their historic periods, these buildings and monuments became part of my own personal history. My photos (some, of course, including us) would say that we had stood at these grand historic sites, adding our own layer of time, making our own imprint. It was a testimony to how much we appreciated these magnificent buildings.

Other followers of Jesus in the past have admired beautiful architecture: *"As Jesus was leaving the temple, one of his disciples said to him, 'Look, Teacher! What massive stones! What magnificent buildings!' "* (Mark 13:1). *"Some of his disciples were remarking about how the temple was adorned with beautiful stones"* (Luke 21:5).

These buildings that were admired were the temple buildings of Jerusalem, a busy city visited by many. Photography had yet to be invented, otherwise I'm sure there would be thousands of annual photos taken by families who yearly travelled to Jerusalem to celebrate the Feast of the Passover.

Jesus didn't condemn his disciples for appreciating architecture and beauty and buildings. Jesus even referred to the buildings as 'great' because they were indeed massive structures. Being God, He knew the human creativity that went into the design of these buildings. Being human, He knew the carpentry, masonry and heavy labour involved in the building of structures.

Jesus also knew this impressive landmark of Jerusalem would be destroyed. *"'Do you see all these great buildings?' replied Jesus. 'Not one stone here will be left on another; every one will be thrown down'"* (Mark 13:2).

Jerusalem would be attacked by the Romans under the rule of Titus in 70 A.D. and the temple would be completely destroyed by fire. Jesus wanted his disciples to be impressed with that which could not be destroyed. In Luke's account, Jesus began His response about the stones with the words, *"As for what you see here"* (Luke 21:6). In other words, what the eye could see was not going to endure.

Like the temple, this world that we see around us will not last. The chapter goes on to describe signs of the second coming of Christ. Jesus said, *"Heaven and earth will pass away, but my words will never pass away"* (Luke 21:33). Even the most enduring things we make today are not made to last into eternity. So those things should not be what impress us the most.

Christ's words, His promises and admonitions will last forever. People will last forever. It is people that we are to view as important because they have eternity ahead of them.

God sees all of my photographs. He knows all about the fabulous building of Notre-Dame, but He is more interested in the man emerging from the left, whom I've cropped out and know nothing about. This is a man made in the image of God. God is well aware of the beauty of Sacré-Coeur up on the hill but His attention is on the person dressed in fluorescent orange, whom He loves and died for.

If God had a photograph of His most precious building, it would be a picture of a building made up of people. No wood, concrete or actual stones involved, just people. It is a perfect and beautiful picture in God's heart.

As you come to him, the living Stone—rejected by humans but chosen by God and precious to him—you also, like living stones, are being built into a spiritual house to be a holy priesthood, offering spiritual sacrifices acceptable to God through Jesus Christ. For in Scripture it says: "See, I lay a stone in Zion, a chosen and precious cornerstone, and the one who trusts in him will never be put to shame."

—I Peter 2:4-6

We are the photograph God has in His heart.

$\mathcal{A}$ daughter, seeing her mother sitting on a bench in the love-ly Luxembourg Gardens, takes a picture. When the moth-er looks at the picture of herself, what does she see? She sees, in contrast to the nearby red and yellow vibrant flowers, a woman sitting on a park bench looking tired, her slouched posture not helping. The white shirt adds to the pale look, confirming that she has been in more museums than sunshine.

This was one of the eight hundred photos on my digital camera. It is not one of my favourite pictures, but then sometimes I can be overly critical of myself. I think we all do that. Sometimes, though, a photo of ourselves grabs our attention, surprising us with pleasant approval. Per-haps it's our hair, eyes, and complexion; everything works well together. It's a pleasant, natural look where nothing in the background looks like it's growing out of our heads. When skimming through my photos, there was one such photo taken at Notre-Dame that I instantly liked.

We visited Notre-Dame early on our second morning together. No-tre-Dame took almost two hundred years to build, between the years 1163-1345. To do justice to this phenomenal building, it deserved photos of its entire perimeter: the supporting flying buttresses, the stained-glass rose windows, the tranquil back gardens, and the intriguing front.

Of the three front carved portals, the central one had Christ seated with both hands raised, judging the good from the evil. Above that, lining the building were what I had thought were twenty-eight sculpted kings of Israel. But altogether, thirty-nine kings ruled the divided kingdoms of Judah and Israel, and so I wondered exactly which kings these were. The answer had to be a Christ-centred one, tracing Christ's lineage through the line of Judah. "*The scepter will not depart from Judah*" (Genesis 49:10). But only twenty kings ruled in Judah.

Further research pointed to these statues representing not individual kings, but twenty-eight generations, spanning the generations from King David to Christ (Matthew 1:17).

The Apostle Paul writes of the importance of Israel in Romans 9:5: "*Theirs are the patriarchs, and from them is traced the human ancestry of the Messiah, who is God over all, forever praised! Amen.*"

Having done some digging, I can now see and appreciate the amazing Christ-centredness in the front of Notre-Dame.

At the time of the French Revolution, when the wealthy monarchy was despised, these kings were mistaken for the kings of France and in the rage against the monarch the sculptures of the kings were decapitated. After the revolution, new heads were sculpted to replace them. Amazingly, in 1977, the original king's heads were discovered and are now displayed in the Musée de Cluny, the National Museum of the Middle Ages.

When Hannah and I arrived at Notre-Dame in the early morning, we took plenty of photos inside as well, walking up one side of the nave and down the other, photos of paintings, sculptures, small chapels and the famous round stained-glass rose windows.

Then we lined up outside along the north sidewalk for the tower tours. Because the tours were restricted to twenty people at a time, we had a fifty-minute wait. Once inside on tour, a narrow spiral marble staircase confronted us immediately. Climbing as a group in very close quarters is great motivation to keep going. Having a woman who was older than me right at my heels kept me putting one foot in front of the other.

The staircase opened up to a gift shop (where it's best not to buy anything too heavy, because more stairs lie ahead). Eventually we climbed to the top, conquering all 402 steps. There we explored the medieval towers of Notre-Dame and took many more photos. It was at the top of Notre-Dame with fantastic views of the city where Hannah took the picture of me that I liked. It became one of my favourites. The views from the top included the Eiffel Tower, the golden dome of the Hôtel des Invalides, the Louvre and the Seine. But none of those magnificent scenes formed any part of the backdrop in this particular picture.

In my photo, forty-six metres above the ground, the background was dull with grey concrete, black iron fencing and grey wire. I wore a black shirt.

Although I had been nervous because of the height, edges and narrow confines, at that particular stretch I was not afraid. We had walked along by the gargoyles of Notre-Dame, designed to protrude from the building for the purpose of draining rainwater. Besides gargoyles, chimeras (designed by Voillet le-Duc in the nineteenth century) had been carved as ornamental statues of mythical birds, creatures or beasts with different animal parts. Many are perched on corners of the balustrades.

In this particular photo, I am standing beside a chimera known as a stryga. According to the visitor's brochure, '*stryga*' is the Greek word for bird of the night. The stryga stands to my right overlooking the streets of Paris. There is an eastern legend which tells of the stryga as a bird that is a nocturnal, evil spirit.

So out of 800 photos, my favourite picture of myself in Paris is the one of me beside a statue representing an evil spirit of the night. I thought about this mild tourist disaster and tried to see it in a different light. The row of kings pointed to Christ and the chimera image somehow had to do the same. I needed to view this photo in an encouraging way. And I found that I could.

I saw it as a picture of a Christian who, having climbed the heights, is now out in the open, unafraid, standing against evil. Isn't that when Christians should look their best—when we're standing, not sitting, with our faith in Christ, standing in His strength, doing His will?

> *Finally, be strong in the Lord and in his mighty power. Put on the full armor of God so that you can take your stand against the devil's schemes… so that when the day of evil comes, you may be able to stand your ground, and after you have done everything, to stand.*
> —Ephesians 6:10-11, 13

"*Resist him [the devil], standing firm in the faith…* " (I Peter 5:9).

The life of ease is not the picture to strive for. Slouching in comfort, feet safely planted on the ground, taking no risks, doing nothing. It really isn't a good picture for the Christian.

Sunset over the Seine

Transitioning Home

> *"Home is the nicest word there is."*
> Laura Ingalls Wilder

> *"He is the happiest, be he king or peasant,*
> *who finds peace in his home."*
> Johann Wolfgang von Goethe

> *"Every house where love abides*
> *And friendship is a guest,*
> *Is surely home, and home sweet home*
> *For there the heart can rest."*
> Henry Van Dyke

$\mathcal{E}$ vening settled over the city on our last night in Paris. The lights on the tree-lined Champs-Élysées brought everything more to life, if that were possible. Paris was called The City of Light initially because it had become a centre of education, philosophy and learning in the eighteenth-century Age of Enlightenment. In 1828, Paris continued to be known as *La Ville-Lumière*, the City of Light, because of the gas lamps installed along the Champs-Élysées, the first city in Europe to use gas street lamps.

Today, Paris is often thought of as the City of Lights (plural) because of the hundreds of lights around monuments, fountains, churches, hotels, statues, bridges and streets. Since December 31, 1985, the Eiffel Tower illuminates sparkling gold in the evenings due to Pierre Bideau's invention of hundreds of projectors with yellow-orange sodium lamps which light the tower from the inside, emphasizing its iron structure. In the evenings, every time the Eiffel Tower came into view if the time was right, Hannah and I would stop to watch, as many others did. For five minutes, every hour on the hour, the tower sparkled and glittered in blue against gold.

With the Place de la Concorde well behind us, we began our stroll along the Champs-Élysées, alerted to well-known designer names. Through huge one- and two-storey high, well lit windows, expert window dressers cleverly displayed trendy clothes, jewelry, purses, and even cars. Window shopping couldn't have been more fun.

Pleasant restaurants enticed us with their warm lights and delicious aromas. We decided upon a restaurant, once again to share a pizza. Our order arrived at the time that the four men next to us finished their meal. Although they left around ten in the evening, still the restaurant bustled with more patrons ready to come in. As soon as the men next to us left, the waiters efficiently cleared the table so that it shone with freshness, smartly placed serviettes, and sparkling wine glasses. But both of us spotted a hint of red under the table. A fallen serviette failed to be noticed. No sooner had the thought entered our minds, a waiter's hand swooped down to retrieve it.

Parisians manage the restaurant business close to perfectly. In all of the restaurants I visited, meals were pleasantly presented and absolutely delicious, and never once, no matter how busy the restaurant, did I ever feel rushed. To dine meant time was purposefully set apart to sit down and to savour every part of the meal beginning to end. In Paris, I realized that any-thing to do with food or drink was not done standing, walking or driving. It's an interesting concept.

After our meal, we continued our walk along the lit Champs-Élysées toward the beaming gold Arc de Triomphe that Napoleon built to commem-orate France's victories and the French armies during his reign. All French armies are remembered now at the Arc de Triomphe. In 1944, Charles de Gaulle and Allied troops marched from here down the Champs-Élysées in triumph, celebrating the liberation of Paris.

The museum at the top of the arch had already closed by the time we got there. In between and around the base of the four pillars, we gazed up at each of the battle reliefs, glowing brilliant gold from the embedded ground lights. The pillars displayed etched lists of generals who served in the wars. We circled the Tomb of the Unknown Soldier from WWI, brightly lit and decorated with flowers.

A security guard informed us and the few other tourists that the site was closing for the evening. A man sleeping with a wine bottle tucked into his jacket had to be roused and he joined us in leaving the premises through the underpass. We came up the steps from the underpass and walked back along the Champs-Élysées, leaving behind the glowing arch of gold.

Those hours of dazzling excitement disappeared the moment we de-scended the steps to the Métro line, and our thoughts turned to packing up and leaving Paris. At some point later in the dark night, switches would be flipped off and automated programs ended as the lights around the city of Paris went out. The sun would rise later and daylight would reign.

Leaving such a dazzling place as the City of Lights, I took comfort knowing I didn't leave all the lights behind. Some lights would follow me no matter where I went and would shine on my side of the world: "*God made two great lights—the greater light to govern the day and the lesser light to govern the night. He also made the stars*" (Genesis 1:16).

God never fails with His lights to bring the sun out, have the moon run its course and the stars take their position. The lights that God controls, we count on daily. These lights are not faulty, not in danger of running into mechanical difficulty and they've never needed upgrades over the millennia.

As constant as they are, they continually surprise us because we never know how clearly the moon will rise or how spectacular the sunrise will appear. "*The sun has one kind of splendor, the moon another and the stars another; and star differs from star in splendor*" (I Corinthians 15:41).

When human-made lights fail to cheer us up or we fail to see God's splendor in His lights in the sky, we need to remember that Christ is the true Light. "*When Jesus spoke again to the people, he said, 'I am the light of the world. Whoever follows me will never walk in darkness, but will have the light of life'*" (John 8:12). He is the Light that will never leave us, that will never fail. He is the only Light that is eternal.

All lights, except Christ, will eventually run their course. A time will come when they will be needed no more. "*There will be no more night. They will not need the light of a lamp or the light of the sun, for the Lord God will give them light*" (Revelation 22:5).

At the hotel that evening, we prepared for the long day of travel awaiting us. My suitcase would go as cargo this time, so size, weight and organization was not an issue for me. I unzipped the top portion to achieve the two-inch expansion and I could help Hannah out by taking some of her things back home. This included the yellow traveller's mug she had found at a shop along Quai des Grands Augustins. It would be perfect for her commute across the city—memories of Paris wrapped up in a yellow traveller's mug of hot chocolate. I stuffed the mug with smaller trinkets, then wrapped it, hoping not to lose another of Hannah's yellow cups. I carefully folded the scarves I bought near the Bastille, and the scarf from the store that we saw along rue de la Huchette.

Morning arrived and became a good time to leave Paris. The lights had been turned off in the City of Lights. The sun shone beautifully on the stones, leaves and water. Ahead lay the hours of travel retracing the familiar paths.

Hannah and I left the hotel around six in the morning, and walked to the Métro station. At Gare du Nord, we hugged goodbye and I watched Hannah head toward the Eurostar entrance for her journey beneath the English Channel back to England before I took the train to the airport.

I checked my suitcase at the airport, leaving me plenty of time to search for a café and relax with one last taste of French pastry in France. Along the wide expanse, I browsed the kiosks and found one selling beautifully packaged macarons. One more perfect gift to bring back for my family. No point in bringing home unnecessary Euros. They would only occupy a box labelled 'foreign coins' that was mostly filled with American pennies, nickels and dimes.

Going home lacked the excitement of heading into the unknown. Intriguing old cobblestone roads and four hundred year old churches didn't exist in Calgary. My vacating had ended and I needed to return to fill the space I had left. But it was returning to a place of belonging, a place I want to be—home. And in that, I anticipated the happiness of returning to family, friends and routines.

Paris soon became a memory as I flew across the Atlantic. I arrived at the Calgary airport, happy to be home and thrilled to see Ian and Philip again. Before I knew it, I found myself back in my home, and unpacked.

The autumn season hadn't arrived in Calgary yet, but leaving Paris seemed to have ushered it in early. The busyness of September waited around the corner to arrive in a week's time. Like the school year beginning in September, the church year was similar, with ministries ready to begin after the summer break. Even around the house, it seemed appropriate to plan a few autumn projects. Areas inside the house could do with some fresh paint. The garden and flower beds needed that change-of-season attention.

But initially, upon returning home from Paris, I did nothing. After my vacation, I relaxed on the couch, snacking away on the macarons I had picked up at Charles de Gaulle airport. I ate only the macarons designated for my son, who turned out not to be fond of them. Philip did like the book I got him from Shakespeare and Company, the rich French chocolates and the t-shirt. I think he fared quite well with his gifts.

Just home from a Paris vacation, lying on the couch, munching macarons—I suppose if I liked soap operas, I'd be watching them. Thoughts of doing any kind of work were just that—only thoughts. It would seem King Solomon had people such as me in mind when he wrote, *"How long will you lie there, you sluggard?"* (Proverbs 6:9)

I'd have an explanation for him. I would tell him about the long walk along the Champs-Élysées on that last night in Paris; combined with the accumulated miles put on over the other eight days. Then the miles at the airports in France and Amsterdam. I'd continue on about the pressurized cabin affecting my circulation. I would throw in the fact that I am not as young as I used to be. Defensively, I would conclude that all these factors have contributed to a situation which has made me only *look* like a sluggard.

What really happened was that I needed time to be still. Time to lie on the couch with my legs raised up above my heart so that the swelling around my ankles would decrease. I really didn't want to visit my doctor so soon again unless absolutely necessary. And it worked wonderfully. After a few days of taking things easy, the swelling decreased significantly.

This was very good because changes were coming. Vacations ended and friends returned. Kids prepared for school. New church ministries and meetings were arranged. Everything breathed preparation. Even the air was changing. It grew cooler in the evenings. The evergreen's shadows stretched out longer. The sun set earlier.

A new season approached quickly. Like harvest time, new work appeared. Workers were needed in the harvest field. *"There is a time for everything, and a season for every activity under the heavens"* (Ecclesiastes 3:1). My vacation was over. Then it was time to get off the couch and move into the next season.

chapter 30
More Time

*W*hen I returned home, a friend asked if I had seen the sailboats in Paris. Immediately, a scene came to mind as if from a movie: a Parisian park where smartly dressed children sailed little boats around in a vast sparkling pool of water on a warm sunny afternoon. What movie could that have been? Noting my searching face, she added that it took place in the Luxembourg Gardens. Having been in that garden several times, but never making it down to the south end, I assumed that the sailing action occurred at that end, and that, therefore, I had missed the boats.

Curious about it, I looked at some sites online and realized that the little boat rental was located at the main basin where I had gone on my first afternoon. Hannah and I had also strolled through the north end of the Luxembourg taking photos. Perhaps boats were not sailing at those times or I simply didn't notice. If I could have spent more time there, I'm sure I would have seen sailboats.

Often our timing doesn't work out. If only we had just a little bit more time, a few more hours, a few more days. This wasn't the only incident when I was close, but not close enough.

After a search through the Latin Quarter, I had triumphantly approached the entrance door of a quilting store tucked away on a quiet street. But the door had been locked. Adjusting my eyes to the darkness through the window only produced outlines of unknown things. Maybe the woman who operated this store had gone for a lunch break. But then again, with everything being so dark, I thought that the store might no longer be in business.

A few metres away, a local man comfortable in his cargo pants and t-shirt, sat on the concrete step. He lifted his arm that rested on his knee, to take the cigarette out of his mouth. "*Probablement elle est en vacances.*"

I hadn't thought of that and replied, "*Ah, mais oui, en vacances.*" I remembered hearing about store owners taking their vacations in August. I left, thinking that if I could hang around Paris a little longer, I would have been able to see this unique store and the fabulous quilting fabrics described on their website.

I also walked away surprised by the conversation. It wasn't lengthy, but it happened so naturally. Maybe he thought I was a local Parisian. With a *joie de vivre* kind of bounce in my step, fanciful thoughts grew about our family packing up everything and moving to Paris. That would be one way to have more time.

After seeing Napoleon Bonaparte's tomb, six caskets within each other, at Les Invalides, Hannah and I had begun our walk towards the Musèe d'Orsay. We had chosen to forego the Musèe Rodin which had just closed. On our way to the d'Orsay, I noticed that the sidewalk was bordered by a black wrought iron fence, inside of which ran an equally high trimmed hedge.

I paused to look at the map because I remembered the Musèe Rodin to be close by and saw that the fence we walked along bordered the Rodin Gardens. Knowing that the entrance to the museum and gardens lay up ahead to the right, I visualized what I recalled from our visit twenty years before. Excitedly, I told Hannah my idea.

"If we can look beyond this fence and hedge, through here somehow, I think *The Thinker* should be really close."

With our cameras between the iron rods, we zoomed in where we found convenient gaps in the hedge. Spots of green lawn appeared.

Zooming in more, we saw him! Not the view most tourists see, but it was unmistakably him—*Le Penseur* (*The Thinker*) from the backside. *The Thinker*, with his broad muscular green back, had his right shoulder curved down, and had the back of his head bent down in contemplation. This sculpture of August Rodin, his work of 1880-1904, perhaps represented Dante, the Italian poet. Spying on *The Thinker* from the back was better than not seeing him at all. But I knew of the famous front view of him that we couldn't see, not to mention all the other marvelous works of Rodin. Had we another day in Paris, the Rodin Museum would certainly be something we would check off our list.

Hannah and I did well, seeing many of the sites that we intended to, and definitely more than we had anticipated. However, until a person arrived in Paris and saw for themselves the intriguing scope of history, architecture and culture every single block in the city had to offer, they wouldn't quite understand that almost painful desire for just a little bit more time. I could write chapters on the things we *didn't* see and do in Paris, and reading between the lines, one would sense my frustration.

Limitations of time are a common frustration and challenge. The Apostle Paul writes it succinctly: *"What I mean, brothers and sisters, is that the time is short"* (I Corinthians 7:29). Our lives here are not long. Our time here is short, not unlike a vacation where endless choices abound about how we will spend that time.

The writer of the book of Hebrews wanted to get the letter written and delivered to its intended recipients, and he was well aware of time restraints. He made choices about what he wrote: *"Above the ark were the cherubim of the Glory, overshadowing the atonement cover. But we cannot discuss these things in detail now"* (Hebrews 9:5).

Further into his letter, he wrote: *"And what more shall I say? I do not have time to tell about Gideon, Barak, Samson and Jephthah, about David and Samuel and the prophets"* (Hebrews 11:32). Names were listed, but no time given to delve into personal details, and surprisingly not even time to note the details of King David. Many great stories of faith and sacrifice could have been recorded, but the writer refrained because he needed to get on to other issues before closing off the letter.

Time constrains us. Every day we wake up to too much. If we've made a list, it is usually too long. We can't possibly do it all, certainly not in a day. We can't do all we want to do, not in our lifetime here. We need to keep in mind, what Jesus said:

> *Come to me, all you who are weary and burdened, and I will give you rest. Take my yoke upon you and learn from me, for I am gentle and humble in heart, and you will find rest for your souls. For my yoke is easy and my burden is light.*
>
> —Matthew 11:28-30

There is a picture of Hannah in the Musée d'Orsay that illustrates this verse. There are views through the huge clock window on the top floor that look out over the Seine and the Right Bank. At the base of the clock sits a collection of large bean-bag chairs, where Hannah sank comfortably down in one, relaxed and at peace.

Time—with its huge demands and constraints—can be a cruel master towering over us. But it is Christ we are to serve. His burden is light, and when we serve Him, we find true rest.

*T*he clip that held up her dark hair still allowed curled strands to fall, meeting the fabric of her dress. Like many French women, she was slim and pretty. She wore petite black high heels. If she was about to walk into the most exquisite restaurant in Paris, she would be graciously welcomed by the *maître d'*. But she was not entering a restaurant.

Early in the morning along Boulevard St. Michel, the shops had yet to open when I saw her. She stood outside one of the shops, with a strong sense of presence. A gold and white jeweled bracelet that glistened in the sun graced her right arm. Below the bracelet, her hand firmly grasped a mop. On the concrete step near her black heels, a pail of grey water waited to become even greyer.

Not long after that morning, I returned home from my vacation in Paris. On a Sunday, soon after arriving home, we went to church. It became one of those busy Sundays where Ian and Philip had prior commitments in the afternoon. I drove home, parked the car in the garage and walked out of the garage door. We have a detached garage so that between the garage and the back door to our house is an open concrete patio area.

As much as I wanted to go inside to prepare some lunch, I stopped and observed our patio area where bits of scattered debris from a recent hailstorm lay. It was not a disaster zone, but it certainly was messy. A strong urge hit me right then and there to clean it up. I glanced down at my black heels. I was trapped. Didn't I need to change my clothes first?

The remembrance of the French woman in black heels with mop in hand barged into my mind, challenging my thinking. *Why can't I? What's stopping me?*

Instead of entering my house, I returned to the garage to retrieve an old broom we keep tucked around the corner by the door. I began sweeping up small twigs, pinecones, leaves and petals. Continuing in my heels, black skirt and teal summer top, I worked my way around the patio furniture, moving chairs and plant pots, sweeping everywhere.

The task took on a strange significance. In the quietness of the sunny backyard, the hawks, magpies and butterflies carried on with their business, taking absolutely no notice of me. Contented and engrossed in my work, I carried on diligently. Time was of no concern. The task became important; it was important that I do a good job, taking no short cuts, doing nothing in a sloppy way.

We had no one coming over that evening for a barbecue; nothing special had been planned. All that mattered was to have the place clean and ready. Being nicely dressed, I wanted the patio to also look nice. As if opening up for a day of business, the place needed to look welcoming and comfortable. The best I could possibly make it.

If only all tasks I do, I do as if I were in heels.

If only all tasks I do, I do my best, because I do them for Christ's glory.

Christ is worthy so that whatever we do, whether a seemingly insignificant unseen task, some big undertaking or something in between, we seek to do our very best. We offer work that is done well, with care and class.

Whatever you do, work at it with all your heart, as working for the Lord, not for human masters, since you know that you will receive an inheritance from the Lord as a reward. It is the Lord Christ you are serving.

—Colossians 3:23-24

I believe that everything we do for Christ now out of joy and our own volition, we will be so very happy that we did those things once we are in heaven. Jesus Christ is what matters above all else. The first command centres on our Lord. "*Love the Lord your God with all your heart and with all*

127

Kim Louise Clarke

your soul and with all your mind. This is the first and greatest commandment"
(Matthew 22:37-38).

After I cleaned up the patio area, wearing my nice clothes and high heels, I went into the house. Later that afternoon, having changed into shorts, t-shirt and flip-flops, I sat outside in the comfy patio chair, sipping a large, dark roast coffee. My private café in the sun.

I thought about my French collection of moments, a unique collection that stood out in a wonderful vacation that had never been interrupted by a migraine. There had been no passing out on the banks of the Seine. No collapsing on a park bench. No need to fear that God would not be close to me. God had certainly upheld me and guided me and I knew He would continue to do so. Wherever I am, I can look forward to many more moments to stand out. I could go on collecting them the rest of my life.

Getting There

St. Augustine - www.brainyquote.com/quotes/topics/topic_travel.html
Roland Gau, Dutch Proverb - www.exploreforayear.com/inspiration/55-quotes-travel

Chapter 1 – Stepping Out in Bijou
www.britannica.com/EBchecked/topic/81281/Phillips-Brooks
www.brainyquote.com (search - Phillip Brooks)

Walking in Gardens

Victor Hugo - Google search: Quotes on Gardens - images
Abraham Lincoln - 2011 Engagement Calendar, New York, Peter Pauper Press, Inc. 2010
Helen Keller - To Love This Life – Quotations by Helen Keller (New York, AFB Press American Foundation for the Blind, 2000)

Chapter 4 - Crossing the Luxembourg
www.senat.fr/visite/jardin/index.html
www.en.parisinfo.com/paris-museum-monument/71393/Jardin-du-Luxembourg
www.aviewoncities.com/paris/saintgermaindespres.htm

www.brittanica.com/EBchecked/topic/219315/French-Revolution
www.sacred-destinations.com/france/paris-st-sulpice
www.lebonmarche.com

Chapter 5 - Trouble in the Tuileries
www.aviewoncities.com/paris/tuileries.htm
www.famouswonders.com/jardin-des-tuileries
www.aviewoncities.com/paris/placedelaconcorde.htm
www.art-quotes.com (Pierre-Auguste Renoir – from Beauty category)

Chapter 6 - Heart for the Eiffel Tower
www.travelfranceonline.com.fountains-place-de-la-concorde-paris
www.aviewoncities.com/paris/placedelaconcorde.htm
www.aviewoncities.com/paris/tuileries.htm
www.art-quotes.com (Claude Monet - from Nature category)
James Strong, *"New Strong's Exhaustive Concordance of the Bible"* (Nashville, Tennessee: Thomas Nelson Publishers, 1984)

Chapter 8 - Daisies and Billy Goats
www.aviewoncities.com/paris/palaisroyal.htm
www.paris.fr/english/parks-woods-gardens-and-cemeteries/gardens/palais-royal/rub_8212_stand_34232_port_18987
www.art-quotes.com (Claude Monet - from Nature category)
www.worldstories.org.uk/stories/story/79-three-billy-goats-gruff

Chapter 9 - Something is Missing
www.paris.fr/english/parks-woods-gardens-and-cemeteries/gardens/palais-royal/rub_8212_stand_34232_port_18987
www.statue-de-paris.sculpturederue.fr

All in a Day

Mike Murdock - www.brainyquote.com/quotes/authors/m/mike_murdock.html
Robert Louis Stevenson - www.art-quotes.com

Author Unknown - Google search: Images for quotes on routine

Chapter 11 - The In-Between Things
www.parisinfo.com/musee-monument-paris/71336/Square-René-Viviani
www.shakespeareandcompany.com

Chapter 12 - Stepping into Curiosity
www.aviewoncities.com/paris/pontneuf.htm

Chapter 13 - Contentment
www.brainyquote.com (search – Phillip Brooks)
James Strong, *"New Strong's Exhaustive Concordance of the Bible"* (Nashville, Tennessee: Thomas Nelson Publishers, 1984)

Lost in the Past

J.R.R. Tolkien, *The Fellowship of the Ring* - www.brainyquote.com/quotes/keywords/lost.html
Danny Kaye - www.brainyquote.com/quotes/topics/topic_travel.html
St. Augustine - www.quotegarden.com/self-discovery.html

Chapter 14 - Lost in the Latin Quarter
www.walkgeneration.com/Paris/ViewWalk
www.writersinparis.com/fromwritersinparis.php
www.sacred-destinations.com/france/paris-st-etienne-du-mont
www.sacred-destinations.com/france/paris-pantheon
www.pleiadegroupparisliterature
Ernest Hemingway, *"A Moveable Feast"* (New York: Charles Scribner's Son, 1964), 3.

Chapter 15 - Number Unknown
www.chanel.com
www.chanel.com/en_US/fragrance-beauty/Fragrance-Women

Chapter 17 - La Cimetière du Père-Lachaise
www.pariscemeteries.com/pages/perelachaise.html

Chapter 18 - Ancient Stones
www.historvius.com/musee-de-cluny-868/
www.britannica.com/EBchecked/topic/507739/Roman-Empire
www.paris.culture.fr/en/
www.discoverfrance.net/France/Paris/Parks_Gardens/Arenes_de_Lutece.shtml

Travelling Together

Ernest Hemingway - www.brainyquote.com/quotes/topics/topic_travel.html
Tim Cahill - Google search: quotes on travel together; images
Robert Louis Stevenson - www.brainyquote.com/quotes/topics/topic_travel.html

Chapter 19 - Reflecting at Rue Rivoli
www.paris1900.lartnouveau.com/paris06/fontaine_st_michel.htm
www.en.parisinfo.com/transport/73150/Fontaine-Saint-Michel

Chapter 20 - The Helicopter
James Strong, *"New Strong's Exhaustive Concordance of the Bible"* (Nashville, Tennessee: Thomas Nelson Publishers, 1984)

Chapter 21 - Sacré-Coeur
www.sacré-coeur-montmartre.com/english/history-and-visit
www.aviewoncities.com/paris/sacrécoeur.htm
www.aviewoncities.com/paris/montmartre.htm
www.sacred-destinations.com/france/paris-sacré-coeur
www.vangoghgallery.com/painting/floral.html
www.artquotes.com   (Vincent van Gogh – from Choices category)
Visitor's Brochure - The Sacred Heart Basilica in Montmartre

Chapter 22 - Beware of Deceit
www.worldsiteguides.com/europe/france/paris/pont-alexandre-iii

Chapter 23 - Yellow Cup Memories
www.toureiffel.paris

Art and Photography

Vincent van Gogh and Leonardo da Vinci - www.goodreads.com/quotes.
tag.art
Ansel Adams - www.brainyquote.com/quotes

Chapter 24 - Armour in the Louvre
www.louvre.fr/en/history-louvre
www.louvre.fr/en/oeuvre-notices/napoleon-battlefield-eylau
www.louvre.fr/en/oeuvre-notices/battle-san-romano

Chapter 25 - Miracles in the Louvre
www.louvre.fr/en/oeuvre-notices/wedding-feast-cana
www.livescience.com31935-louvre-museum.html

Chapter 26 - Great Buildings
www.sacred-destinations.com/france/paris-saint-chapelle

Chapter 27 - The Stryga
www.notredamedeparis.fr/spip.php?article381
www.notredamedeparis.fr/spip.php?article383
Visitor's Brochure - Towers of Notre-Dame (Centre des monuments
nationaux, Paris)

Transitioning Home

Laura Ingalls Wilder - www.goodreads.com/quotes/tag/home?page=2
Johann Wolfgang von Goethe - www.verybestquotes.com/quotes-about-
home/#sthash.FEzhjc6i.dpuf

Henry Van Dyke - www.verybestquotes.com/quotes-about-home/#st-hash.FEzhjc6i.dpuf

Chapter 28 - Along the Champs-Élysées

www.mtholyoke.edu/courses/rschwart/hist255-s01
www.aviewoncities.com/paris/arcdetrioumphe
www.arcdetriompheparis.com
www.travelsignposts.com/France/sightseeing/interesting-facts-par-is-lights
www.caloundracity.asn.au/Francofiles/paris/paris-ligt.html
www.toureiffel.paris

Chapter 30 - More Time
www.musee-armee.fr/en/collections/museum-spaces/dome-des-inva-lides-tomb-of-napoleon-i.html
www.rodinmuseum.org/collections/permanent/1-3355.html
www.parisdigest.com/takingarest/jardindu.htm